Look Again!
Appealing Bulletin Boards
for Secondary Students

By Judy Serritella

A Publication of THE BOOK REPORT & LIBRARY TALK

Linworth Publishing, Inc.
Worthington, Ohio

Library of Congress Cataloging-in-Publication Data

Published by Linworth Publishing, Inc.
480 East Wilson Bridge Road, Suite L
Worthington, Ohio 43085

Copyright © 2002 by Linworth Publishing, Inc.

1-58683-053-8

5 4 3 2 1

Table of Contents

Table of Contents

Table of Contents

Table of Contents

Dedication

This book is dedicated to my husband, Dan, who has always encouraged and believed in me. It is also dedicated to my friend "Grandma" Helen Walker, who died in 2001. She wrote the following poem when she was eight years old:

Books
Books are a pleasure
To all mankind
They fill with knowledge
The hungry mind.

And besides teaching you
Many things,
They supply pleasure
Fit for a king.

To sit in a cozy corner
Or nook
And in my lap
Have an interesting book

Is all I need for my happiness
To be complete
Because a good book
Is indeed a treat.

—Helen Walker
 Age 8
 1927

Acknowledgements

I would like to thank the Georgia Library Media Association for the grant that initiated this project, the staff at Linworth Publishing for their support and help with this adventure, my colleagues for their inspiration, my friends for their encouragement, and my family for their faith. I would also like to thank Becky McQueen and Sherry Hall, and library media specialists and teachers throughout the world who have sent ideas and suggestions for inventive and inspiring bulletin boards. Those ideas not credited to an individual are the author's ideas.

I would especially like to thank my husband, Dan, and my children, Craig and Maggie, for their encouragement and confidence in me.

About the Author

Judy Serritella grew up in Jacksonville, Florida, and graduated from Georgia College in Milledgeville. She taught the fifth grade for several years and received her master's degree in Library Media from Georgia State University, after which she worked as a media specialist at the elementary and secondary levels.

Currently, Serritella is a library media specialist at Lovejoy High School in Clayton County, Georgia, where she sponsors student council, organizes Homecoming and half-time activities, and has coordinated a project to encourage patriotism. She also is pursuing a specialist degree at the State University of West Georgia.

Serritella is active in a number of professional organizations, including the American Library Association, the National Education Association, the Georgia Library Media Association, the Georgia Association of Instructional Technology, the Georgia Association of Education, and the educational sorority Delta Kappa Gamma. In addition, she is a trustee of the Clayton County public library system.

Her faculty has named her Educator of the Month several times, and she was chosen as the 2001 Georgia Media Specialist of the Year. The faculty and student body additionally honored her by dedicating the yearbook to her.

Married to a psychologist, Serritella and her husband have two children. Their son is a computer integration developer, and their daughter is a student at the State University of West Georgia.

Introduction

ibrary media specialists continually seek effective ways to encourage reading and promote the library media center. Creative and clever bulletin boards can help students gain understanding, inspiration and amusement. Finding these creative ideas is never an easy task. Secondary library media specialists are busy with cataloging, student research projects, and teaching. Often there is little time in a library media specialist's day to think about and plan interesting and appealing bulletin boards. Secondary students do not like elementary-style bulletin boards; they want something that appeals to their age bracket, their interests, and their needs. Although the bulletin board ideas included in this book were originally designed for high school aged students, they can be easily adapted and used in middle school library media centers and classrooms, and in public libraries.

The concept for this book originated from a grant-funded Web site (<www.ccps.ga.net/bulletinboards>) that featured bulletin board ideas designed for secondary students. Colleagues on listservs spread the word. Wonderful ideas poured in from not only the United States, but from all over the world. They were sent to the site, then posted on the Internet. Linworth Publishing saw the site, and a book was born. There are many volumes and numerous Web sites on bulletin board ideas, but most are aimed at elementary students rather than at secondary school students. This book suggests bulletin board and display-case ideas and projects that would appeal to teenagers, yet be simple enough for harried middle or high school library media specialists or teachers to generate.

One of a media specialist's goals is to help students develop lifetime library habits, but, first, students have to come into the library media center. By exhibiting attractive and stimulating bulletin boards, you may draw more students to the media center.

Each bulletin board discussed in this book begins with a concept. The required materials are listed, and some of the ideas are illustrated. Be creative with the backgrounds, borders, captions, and content of your boards. For example, borders can be precut and purchased, or they can be old photographs that the yearbook staff does not want, old or blank CD-ROMs, or designs cut from a letter or die-cut machine. Three-dimensional bulletin boards are always more interesting than one-dimensional ones. Make use of a digital camera, and, as often as possible, use pictures of students and faculty members. Ask community members to donate prizes to motivate students to research interactive bulletin boards.

The chapters are divided into areas of interest and topics that will work in a school setting. While aimed specifically at the secondary level, many of these ideas can be adapted for use at the elementary grade level.

The first chapter, "Get Your Bulletin Board Noticed," is a compilation of bulletin board tips and ideas for eye-catching backings, borders, colors, and lettering. It also suggests some time-saving hints for busy library media specialists. "Author! Author!" focuses on bulletin board ideas about writers. "Beginnings, Endings, and Special Events" spotlights the first and last weeks of school and unusual school events. "The Bookstore" takes specific titles or characters from a book and builds a bulletin board around them. "Catchy Captions" lists amusing, age-appropriate or thought-provoking titles. "Cultural Diversity" describes ways to incorporate bulletin board ideas featuring different ethnic groups. "Dewey Rules" takes specific numbers or groups of numbers in the Dewey Decimal System and develops an idea around them. The "Interactive" chapter suggests ways to use library materials to create questions, quizzes, and entertaining ideas that will attract more patrons. "Research Rules" uses ideas from the Big6™, as well as other ideas, to help students compose term papers, bibliographies, and research papers. "Seasons and Holidays" provides seasonal ideas, while "Strictly Teenagers" contains ideas that probably would appeal only to secondary students. "Technology" has ideas about the computer passwords and the information superhighway. The "Quotations" chapter contains quotes from celebrities, writers, and others about libraries, books, and reading. A bulletin board can be developed around a quote, or quotes can be used in newsletters and pamphlets or made into banners to hang in your library media center. The appendix includes a sample set of stencils, a calendar of events throughout the year, and models of some of the bulletin boards ideas referred to in this book.

Take each of these ideas and make it your own. Use your creativity and talent. Make use of student talent. Add to these ideas, give them your personality, and then watch the students' interest grow in your media center. Recycle your bulletin boards each year, updating books and Web sites, as an ongoing public relations tool for your library media center.

Get Your Bulletin Boards Noticed

CHAPTER 1

L et's get started! Now that you know how this book was developed and what types of bulletin boards it includes, we will delve into specific tips, ideas, and suggestions to help you ensure that your bulletin boards will be noticed and appreciated. Feel free to select from the lists provided and adapt the ideas to fit your particular needs. Enjoy the process of creating lively, interesting bulletin boards that will make secondary students "look again" and attract them to your library media center. Good luck!

BASIC TIPS

- Plan your bulletin boards in advance.
- Begin to collect materials that will help you plan creative bulletin boards.
- Create displays and bulletin boards that will remain up for a least a month.
- Find reliable students to help you make and set up the boards.
- Make sure your theme is instantly clear to the students.
- Make sure the display or bulletin board is neat and organized

BACKINGS

- Cover your bulletin board with fabric; it remains bright and colorful much longer than paper. A wide variety of patterned fabrics are available, and solid fabrics may give you a wider selection of colors than would paper. Denim is sure to be a hit with teenagers and will give you a three-dimensional effect. Using fabric instead of paper saves trees. Fabric can be washed, stored, and reused.
- Wallpaper is another option for bulletin board backing. It comes in a variety of textures, grains, and colors. Wallpaper stores usually have a clearance rack where you can purchase paper at a much-reduced rate.

- Cover your bulletin board with newspaper or the covers of magazines. The Sunday comics provide an especially colorful and amusing background.
- Use brown paper bags from the grocery store.
- For really unusual effects, try using any of the following materials: aluminum foil, artificial grass, old bed sheets, paper or vinyl tablecloths, or bubble wrap (although, if your bulletin board is easily accessible, you should consider the consequences of using the latter material).
- Wrapping paper is another excellent alternative. The ALA produces a beautiful, light-green wrapping paper covered by the word "book" written in different languages. This paper makes an outstanding background.
- Trash bags make an interesting background, especially for bulletin boards that focus on recycling.
- Old paneling or pieces of wooden fences add dimension and interest, and certainly are eye-catching.
- Try file folders, corrugated cardboard, or felt.
- Paint! Remember, however, that this treatment will be permanent, so consider the pros and cons before picking up a paintbrush.
- Use contact paper. (This will be a permanent addition, too, so think about it carefully.)
- Three-dimensional objects, backgrounds, and letters add visual interest.
- Use your imagination.

COLORS

- Use different colors to bring to mind a season; for instance, use holiday colors.
- Use color for different subject matters. For example, red, green, and black would be appropriate for Black History Month. Homecoming bulletin boards should use school colors or colors that suggest "royalty."
- Use eye-catching colors.

BORDERS

- "Store-bought" borders are always an option. They come in many colors and are great time savers.
- Doing a technology-themed board? Use old CDs as a border. Ask students and teachers to donate old or damaged CDs, or ask at music stores (many stores give CDs away). You will have more than enough.
- Do you have access to a letter-cutting machine, such as Ellison™? They create wonderful shapes and borders that can be laminated and used for many years.
- For a school-themed border, use the school's initials.
- Movie ticket stubs can be glued to cardboard and laminated. This is an especially effective border to use with the "You Can't Judge a Book by Its Movie" and "Reel Alternatives" themes.
- Strips of newspaper that are glued to cardboard and laminated make an interesting border.
- Wrapping paper and old greeting cards also can be glued to cardboard or construction paper and laminated.
- Try using the covers of discarded paperback books, cut to the same size.
- Use wide ribbon.

- Ask the yearbook and school newspaper staff for old pictures of students, events, and activities: Students love to see themselves on the bulletin board.
- Use pages from small desk calendars. Cut off the dates if you wish, then glue the pages to cardboard, laminate, and use.
- Old puzzle pieces, play money from board games, or postage stamps make intriguing borders, as do old (or new) postcards.

LETTERING

- Make sure your letters complement your board. Styles, colors, and size are important factors to keep in mind when creating your bulletin board. The size of letters should be proportional to the size of the board or display case; smaller boards = smaller letters. Three-inch letter stencils are included in the appendix.
- Ellison makes letter-cutting devices with an extensive collection of dies.
- Laminating your letters will prevent fading and enable you to use them several times.
- For a three-dimensional look cut duplicate large letters, then staple them together, leaving an opening. Stuff with tissue paper.
- Instead of cutting out individual letters, you may want to use a word-processing program to create lettering.
- Write directly on a background with chalk to create an interesting effect. A light coat of hair spray helps keep the chalk from smearing.
- Keep your caption brief and easy to read from a distance.
- Make sure your letters contrast with, but complement, the background.
- Using two different colors of paper (or whatever material you are using) and gluing them together makes a shadow effect.
- Use straight pins instead of staples to create three-dimensional letters: Pull the letters out from the board to the head of the pin.

TIME-SAVING TIPS

- If you cut out letters to use on your bulletin board, this basic set of letters should last the entire school year:

  A-10 B-4 C-4 D-3 E-14 F-4 G-4 H-6 I-10 J-4 K-4 L-4 M-3 N-10 O-8 P-4 Q-3 R-8 S-8 T-8 U-5 V-3 W-3 X-3 Y-3 Z-2

  A set of stencils is located in the appendix.

CHAPTER 2

Beginnings, Endings and Special Events

ALL IN DUE TIME

THE IDEA
To let students know that the school year is ending and all books must be returned to the library media center by a certain deadline.

THE MATERIALS: Cover the bulletin board with black paper and add the caption "All in due time." Place the final due date in the center of the board, in large letters and numbers. Scatter due-date slips around the board to emphasize that the books need to be returned. You may want to create a large calendar as the background for the bulletin board with "The Due Date" day circled.

See appendix for an example of this bulletin board. (Chart C)

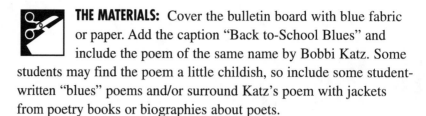

THE IDEA
To showcase a poem in order to welcome students back to school.

THE MATERIALS: Cover the bulletin board with blue fabric or paper. Add the caption "Back to-School Blues" and include the poem of the same name by Bobbi Katz. Some students may find the poem a little childish, so include some student-written "blues" poems and/or surround Katz's poem with jackets from poetry books or biographies about poets.

Back to School Blues

Just wiggling my toes in my brand new shoes
Guess I've got a case of the back to school blues.
Shiny new notebook with nothing inside it
Feeling kinda scared and trying hard to hide it.
I've got three sharp pencils I never used before
And a teacher I don't know behind a classroom door.
Maybe she's a nice one.
Maybe she's bad news.
Just a wiggling and a jiggling to the back to school blues.
—Bobbi Katz

BE A HAPPY CAMPER

THE IDEA
To promote books and materials on camping, hiking, and other outdoor activities.

THE MATERIALS: Cover the bulletin board with blue paper or fabric for the sky; add a lot of trees and a tent. Add the caption "Be a Happy Camper" and attach book jackets that deal with camping, fishing, hunting, hiking, and other outside activities.

See appendix for an example of this bulletin board. (Chart Q)

CAMEO APPEARANCES

THE IDEA
To spotlight important women during Women's History Month and to challenge the students and staff to figure out who is in the spotlight.

THE MATERIALS: Cut six cameos from ivory-colored construction paper, six small ovals from pastel construction paper, and six large ovals from black construction paper. Glue each cameo to the front of a small oval; then glue the left side to the front of a larger oval. Inside the completed cameo, glue a "Who am I?" clue. Attach the cameos to the bulletin board. Cut a large heart shape from pink construction paper. On the front of the heart create a message about the importance of women in society, government, medicine, education, etc. After the bulletin board has been up a while, place the answers under the cameos.

Suggested women and clues:

- Toni Morrison: Noble Prize for Literature 1993
- Alice Walker: Notable author. Wrote *The Color Purple.*
- Agatha Christie: Author of 67 novels, 150 short stories, and 16 plays
- Mother Teresa: Humanitarian. Lived most of her life in Calcutta, India.
- Margaret Chase Smith: First woman to run for President

See appendix for an example of this bulletin board. (Chart I)
Idea suggested by Sandra Sparks, Morrow (Georgia) High School

CHECKOUT THOSE COVERS!

THE IDEA
To introduce teachers and staff members by associating each teacher with a book related to his or her job.

THE MATERIALS: Cover the bulletin board with a bright color or paper. Add the caption "Checkout These Covers!" Using books from your collection and photographs of staff members, place each photo on a book cover, along with the teacher's or staff member's name. An English teacher could be found on the cover of *The A + Guide to Grammar;* the custodian on the cover of a book dealing with hazardous waste; the in-school suspension teacher on the cover of *Doing Time.* Use your imagination and spotlight as many faculty and staff members as possible.

Idea suggested by Carol Burbridge, Jardine Middle School, Topeka, Kansas

EXPEDITION: READ

THE IDEA
To promote reading and your library media center through an outdoors theme.

THE MATERIALS: Cover the bulletin board with burlap, brown fabric, or brown paper. Add the caption "Expedition: Read." Include a person who's wearing outdoor gear and trekking through a rain forest, jungle, or desert. Attach book jackets that are appropriate for the setting. This board would be appropriate for the end of the year.

Idea suggested by Monica McQueen, Eton School, Bellevue, Washington

GRAND OPENINGS EVERY DAY

THE IDEA
A great way to start a new year—have a "Grand Opening." But every day can be a great opening, just open a book.

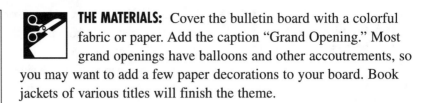

THE MATERIALS: Cover the bulletin board with a colorful fabric or paper. Add the caption "Grand Opening." Most grand openings have balloons and other accoutrements, so you may want to add a few paper decorations to your board. Book jackets of various titles will finish the theme.

HIGH SCHOOLAPOLOOZA

THE IDEA
To welcome new students and returning students, create a bulletin board that uses teenage jargon. Add the name of your school to the caption, for example, "Central High Schoolapolooza" or "Jackson High Schoolapolooza." This bulletin board will inform new students about some of the school's activities and remind the returning students of clubs, events, and activities.

THE MATERIALS: A background of school colors would be appropriate for this bulletin board. Add your appropriate caption. Collect pictures from past school years, from either your own collection or the yearbook. You could include book jackets that feature coping with high school, making friends, and study skills.

HOMECOMING: THEN AND NOW

THE IDEA
To remind students that styles change and people change, but homecoming and spirit are high school constants.

THE MATERIALS: Cover your bulletin board with paper in your school colors. The caption should read, "Homecoming: Then and Now." Place the word "Then" on one side of the board and the word "Now" on the other side. Under "Then," post pictures of your school's past homecomings. Add pictures from faculty members who were on the Homecoming Court when they were in school. Under "Now," include pictures of students who are currently on the homecoming court. This bulletin board will be a hit with faculty, students, and visitors.

See appendix for an example of this bulletin board. (Chart J)

Idea suggested by Kathy Edwards, secretary, Lovejoy (Georgia) High School

IT'S TIME TO HIT THE BOOKS

THE IDEA
To welcome students back to school and remind them that it is time to open those textbooks, library books, and reference materials.

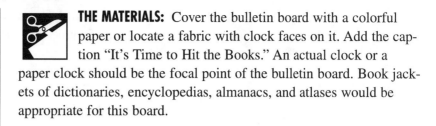

THE MATERIALS: Cover the bulletin board with a colorful paper or locate a fabric with clock faces on it. Add the caption "It's Time to Hit the Books." An actual clock or a paper clock should be the focal point of the bulletin board. Book jackets of dictionaries, encyclopedias, almanacs, and atlases would be appropriate for this board.

LET'S KICK OFF A GREAT YEAR

THE IDEA
To welcome students and staff and to promote the football team of your school.

THE MATERIALS: Cover the bulletin board with fabric or paper in one of your school's colors. Add the caption "Let's Kick Off a Great Year" in the corresponding color. Pictures of the school football team, a large drawing of a foot kicking a ball, or book jackets about football would be appropriate for this board.

NOW ACCEPTING NEW PATRONS

THE IDEA
To encourage students and staff to use the library media center by using advertising, as a business would.

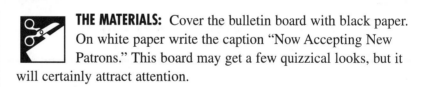

THE MATERIALS: Cover the bulletin board with black paper. On white paper write the caption "Now Accepting New Patrons." This board may get a few quizzical looks, but it will certainly attract attention.

READ BETWEEN THE LINES

THE IDEA
To promote the library media center by featuring your school's football team.

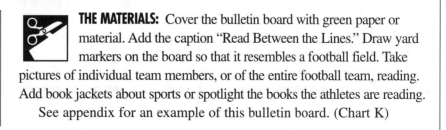

THE MATERIALS: Cover the bulletin board with green paper or material. Add the caption "Read Between the Lines." Draw yard markers on the board so that it resembles a football field. Take pictures of individual team members, or of the entire football team, reading. Add book jackets about sports or spotlight the books the athletes are reading. See appendix for an example of this bulletin board. (Chart K)

SUMMER READING

THE IDEA
To promote reading during the summer months with a *Grease* theme.

THE MATERIALS: Cover the board with bright fabric or paper. Add the caption "Summer Reading" and below the caption add:

"Summer reading, had me a blast.
"Summer reading happened so fast.
"I met a book I'm crazy for…"

Add book jackets or lists of titles for summer reading. Teachers and students may have suggestions for the list.

Idea suggested by Monica McQueen, Eton School, Bellevue, Washington

SUMMER'S A BUMMER WITHOUT A BOOK

THE IDEA
To promote summer reading.

THE MATERIALS: Cover the board with bright fabric or paper. A bright blue background for water, brown paper or fabric for sand, and a bright red sun create a beach scene. A colorful beach ball, placed off center, adds color and interest to your board. Attach jackets of books that you feel students would enjoy reading during the hot summer months. Your AP teachers will have summer reading lists, and other teachers also may suggest titles for this board.

Idea suggested by Monica McQueen, Eton School, Bellevue, Washington

WANT TO LEARN HOW TO PASS?

THE IDEA
During football season use your favorite players to promote the library media center.

THE MATERIALS: Cover the bulletin board with green paper or material. Add the caption "Want to Learn How to Pass?" Draw yard lines on the green paper to resemble a football field. Take pictures of several football players reading their favorite books and place the pictures on the bulletin board "field."

WE ALL WELCOME YOU

THE IDEA
To let students, parents, and visitors know that they are welcome in your school.

THE MATERIALS: Depending upon the size of your school and staff, take a picture of each faculty and staff member. If your school is small, you may want to take individual pictures, while if your school is large, you may want to group the faculty by grade level or subject area. The pictures should be mounted on the bulletin board with the caption "We All Welcome You." Names and/or subject areas can be placed under the pictures. This is a good way to welcome new students and to let everyone learn who's who.

WE WERE YOUNG ONCE

THE IDEA
To introduce students to the teachers and staff, create a bulletin board of photographs of the faculty in their youth. Teachers can provide school pictures or pictures from their yearbooks or childhood.

THE MATERIALS: Cover the board with bright paper or fabric. Have teachers submit a picture of themselves from their youth or childhood, as well as the title of their favorite book at that time of their life. It is a good idea to make copies of the teachers' photographs and use the copies on the board. The students and staff can try to guess who is who, or to match teachers with their favorite book.

Idea suggested by Lillian Hairston, Owings Mill (Maryland) High School

WELCOME TO THE MEDIA CENTER

THE IDEA
To welcome students to the library media center in a variety of languages.

THE MATERIALS: Cover the bulletin board with colorful paper. In the center of the board place the caption "Welcome to the media center." Surround the English words with the same sentiment written in different languages. You may use languages spoken at your school or choose from the phrases listed below:

- Visita, Biblioteca! (Romanian)
- Visitare la bibliotecha! (Italian)
- Käydä Katsomassakirjasto! (Finnish)
- Visitez la bibliotheque! (French)
- Besøge biblioteker! (Danish)
- Besuchen Sie die Bibliothek! (German)
- Ziryaret kütüphamel! (Turkish)
- Bezoeken Zi de lesszaal! (Dutch)
- Visiten la bibliotechaa! (Spanish)
- Wizytowac biblioteka! (Polish)
- Navstiviti knihorna! (Czech)

WHAT I WISH I HAD KNOWN

THE IDEA
In September, greet freshmen with a bulletin board chock-full of advice from older students.

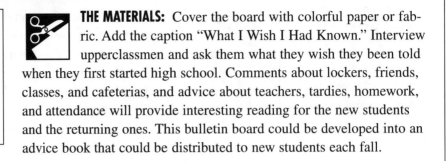

THE MATERIALS: Cover the board with colorful paper or fabric. Add the caption "What I Wish I Had Known." Interview upperclassmen and ask them what they wish they been told when they first started high school. Comments about lockers, friends, classes, and cafeterias, and advice about teachers, tardies, homework, and attendance will provide interesting reading for the new students and the returning ones. This bulletin board could be developed into an advice book that could be distributed to new students each fall.

Seasons and Holidays

CHAPTER 3

BATTY ABOUT BOOKS

THE IDEA
To promote the library media center during the Halloween season.

THE MATERIALS: Cover the board with green fabric or paper. Cut out a large pumpkin or jack-o'-lantern, as well as a lid. Place the lid off to the side. Cut out several black bats and scatter some of them around the bulletin board as if they were flying out of the jack-o'-lantern. The remainder of the bats should be placed around the bulletin board. Write a book title on each bat with white marker. The caption "Batty about Books" should be prominently displayed at the top of the board.

BEST WITCHES

THE IDEA
To promote books that include witches during the Halloween season.

THE MATERIALS: Cover the bulletin board with black or orange paper. Add the caption "Best Witches." Include book jackets or titles that contain witches. Use books from your own collection or choose some from the list below:

- *Macbeth*/Shakespeare
- *The Witch of Blackbird Pond*/Spear
- *The Lion, the Witch and the Wardrobe*/Lewis
- *The Wizard of Oz*/Baum
- *The Witches*/Dahl
- *Harry Potter*/Rowling
- *Enter Three Witches*/Gilmore
- *Tituba of Salem Village*/Petry
- *Summer of Fear*/Duncan
- *The Once and Future King*/White
- *Witch Baby*/Block

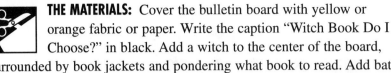

WITCH BOOK DO I CHOOSE?

THE IDEA
To add a touch of whimsy to an October/ Halloween bulletin board.

THE MATERIALS: Cover the bulletin board with yellow or orange fabric or paper. Write the caption "Witch Book Do I Choose?" in black. Add a witch to the center of the board, surrounded by book jackets and pondering what book to read. Add bats, cats, cauldrons, or other Halloween elements to spice up the board.

CURL UP WITH A MYSTERY

THE IDEA
To promote an interest in mystery books, especially during the Halloween season.

THE MATERIALS: Cover the board with colorful fabric. Add the caption "Curl Up with a Mystery." Cut out the silhouette of a person sitting in a chair, feet propped up and reading a book. Place a cutout lamp behind the chair, so that it illuminates the reader. Add book jackets from mystery, detective, and crime titles.

GHOUL'S GALLERY

THE IDEA
To create interest in the library media center during the Halloween season.

THE MATERIALS: Cover the bulletin board with orange paper. This Halloween bulletin board uses a computer image-morphing program to combine two digital pictures into one. Morph library club members, library aides, students, and staff into classic movie monsters. Combine these pictures with scary book jackets into a "Ghoul's Gallery" display for Halloween.

Idea suggested by Brian Regan, East Rochester (New York) High School

HOPE YOUR HOLIDAY IS GRINCH FREE!

THE IDEA
Even secondary students love the Grinch, and everyone loves the holiday season.

THE MATERIALS: Cover the bulletin board with large red-and-white diagonal stripes to resemble a giant candy cane. Write the caption "Hope Your Holiday Is Grinch Free" in green. Place a tree in the center of the board. Cut small pictures of books out of catalogs to "decorate" the tree, along with colored paper balls. Cut out bright, neon-colored paper "lights" for the border. Draw the Grinch's hand and place it in a Santa sleeve, then stuff the sleeve with tissue paper to make it three-dimensional. Complete the Grinch-free bulletin board with "packages" cut from wallpaper, craft paper, and Christmas wrapping paper.

THERE'S SNOW BETTER TIME TO READ

THE IDEA
A catchy title for a January or February bulletin board in the northern climates or for those just wishing for a little snow.

THE MATERIALS: Cover the bulletin board with blue paper. Add the caption "There's Snow Better Time to Read" in white letters. An intricately cut snowflake can replace the letter "o" in "snow." Glue balls of cotton on the board to simulate snow and add seasonal book jackets or titles.

Idea suggested by Martha Zarikow, Information Specialist

BOOKS YULE LOVE TO READ

THE IDEA
To stimulate interest in the library media center during the holiday season.

THE MATERIALS: Cover the bulletin board with black paper. If possible, use real holiday lights to make a border or, if not, create a colorful border of red-and-green paper lights. Write the words "Books Yule Love to Read" in a combination of the holiday colors. Add holiday-themed book jackets or covers for a festive board.

Idea suggested by Sadie Longood, Dallas (Oregon) High School

NO L

THE IDEA
TTo join in the holiday spirit, while encouraging students and staff to use their imaginations.

THE MATERIALS: Cover the bulletin board with strips of red and white paper. Cut out a large letter "L" and place it in the center of the board. Cut out a large circle from black paper, then cut the center out of the circle. Place it over the "L." (Use a pencil and a string to make a nice round circle.) Place a diagonal black strip across the circle to indicate the universal symbol for "No." The bulletin board now says "No L" ("Noel"). Put sprigs of holly in the corners of the board to add pizzazz.

Idea suggested by Kathy Edwards, library media secretary, Lovejoy (Georgia) High School

KEEPING KWANZAA

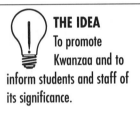

THE IDEA
To promote Kwanzaa and to inform students and staff of its significance.

THE MATERIALS: Cover the board with large strips of black, red, and green paper or fabric, to symbolize the African flag. Black stands for the people, red for struggle, and green for the future and hope that comes from struggle. Add the Kwanzaa principles:

■ *Umoja*: unity
■ *Kujichagulia*: self-determination
■ *Ujama*: cooperative economics
■ *Kuumba*: creativity
■ *Ujima*: collective work and responsibility
■ *Nia*: purpose
■ *Imani*: faith

You can add book jackets about African-American heritage and Kwanzaa.

A NEW HAND FOR A NEW YEAR

THE IDEA
To promote the New Year and encourage reading.

THE MATERIALS: Cover the bulletin board with colorful fabric or paper. Add the caption "A New Hand for a New Year." Purchase large playing cards from a party supply or paper store, and arrange five to seven cards in the form of a "hand," as if you were playing cards. (Tape the cards securely together on the backside so that they do not shift in the display.) Place one to three "hands" in the background with the caption.

Idea suggested by Carol Burbridge, Jardine Middle School, Topeka, Kansas

GREAT LOVERS OF THE WORLD

THE IDEA
To promote the reading of biographies of humanitarians, environmentalists, and social reformers.

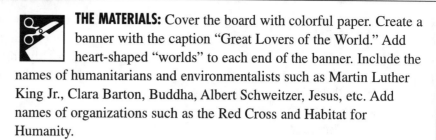

THE MATERIALS: Cover the board with colorful paper. Create a banner with the caption "Great Lovers of the World." Add heart-shaped "worlds" to each end of the banner. Include the names of humanitarians and environmentalists such as Martin Luther King Jr., Clara Barton, Buddha, Albert Schweitzer, Jesus, etc. Add names of organizations such as the Red Cross and Habitat for Humanity.

See appendix for an example of this bulletin board. (Chart P)

Idea suggested by Cindy Pierce, Sky View Middle School, Bend, Oregon

SWEETHEARTS OF LITERATURE

THE IDEA
Spotlight famous "Sweethearts of Literature" on your February bulletin board.

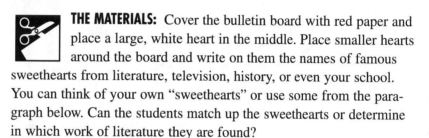

THE MATERIALS: Cover the bulletin board with red paper and place a large, white heart in the middle. Place smaller hearts around the board and write on them the names of famous sweethearts from literature, television, history, or even your school. You can think of your own "sweethearts" or use some from the paragraph below. Can the students match up the sweethearts or determine in which work of literature they are found?

Adam & Eve, Frederic & Catherine from *A Farewell to Arms*, Odysseus & Penelope, Priscilla & John, Tom & Sophy from *Tom Jones*, Heathcliff & Catherine from *Wuthering Heights*, Antony & Cleopatra, Jane & Rochester from *Jane Eyre*, Fred & Wilma, Scarlett & Rhett from *Gone With the Wind*, Jay & Daisy from *The Great Gatsby*, Samson & Delilah, Anna Karenina & Count Dronsky, Emily & George from *Our Town*, Guinivere and Arthur, Lucy & Charles from *A Tale of Two Cities*, Tom & Becky from *Tom Sawyer*, Yurri & Lara from *Dr. Zhivago*, Romeo & Juliet, Elizabeth & Robert Browning, Roxane & Cyrano, Beauty & the Beast, Mickey & Minnie.

GO FLY A KITE!

THE IDEA
To promote the library media center during March, capture the student's attention with a colorful kite bulletin board.

THE MATERIALS: Cover the bulletin board with light-blue paper. Purchase several colorful kites and attach them to the board. Allow one kite to "fly" off of the board by placing it at the edge of the board and partially on the wall. To create kite tails, use colored yarn or twisted strips of tissue paper. Include a poem about kites, such as the one below, and kite-making books.

How the little kite learned to fly.
"I never can do it," the little kite said,
As he looked at the others high over his head;
"I know I should fall if I tried to fly."
"Try," said the big kite; "only try!"
Or I fear you never will learn at all."
But the little kite said, "I'm afraid I'll fall."

The big kite nodded: "Ah well, good-by;
I'm off," and he rose toward the tranquil sky.
Then the little kite's paper stirred at the sight,
And trembling he shook himself free for flight.
First whirling and frightened, then braver grown,
Up, up he rose through the air along,
Till the big kite looking down could see
The little one rising steadily.

Then how the little kite thrilled with pride,
As he sailed with the big kite side by side!
White far below he could see the ground,
And the boys like small spots moving round.
They rested high in the quiet air,
And the birds and the clouds were there.
"Oh, how happy I am!" the little kite cried,
"And all because I was brave, and tried."
     —*Henry Wadsworth Longfellow*

Idea suggested by Sandra Sparks, Morrow (Georgia) High School

FISHING FOR A GOOD BOOK?

THE IDEA
To promote spring or summer reading with a fishing theme. This inspired bulletin board was first created for a display case.

THE MATERIALS: The background is blue fabric or paper. Perch an old pair of blue jeans on paper columns to resemble a dock; add a fishing pole and plastic fish. Add green plants to the background to suggest being under the water. Add fishing-themed book jackets to this display.

Idea suggested by Holly Spanier, Osseo (Minnesota) Junior High School

IF YOU CAN'T STAND THE HEAT

THE IDEA
This caption encourages students to enter your cool, welcoming library during warm summer months.

THE MATERIALS: Cover the bulletin board with red fabric or paper. Add a bright yellow sun, to provide warmth, and the caption, "If You Can't Stand the Heat…Come Into the Media Center…and Read a Cool Book." Add book jackets from your summer reading lists. You could also use jackets of titles set in cold climes or in winter.
See appendix for an example of this bulletin board. (Chart O)

THE IDEA
To promote famous writers who were also fathers.

THE MATERIALS: Cover the bulletin board with dark fabric or paper. Add the caption "Dad's Day." This board works at any time during the year, but is particularly appropriate around Father's Day. Use information from your library media center about famous fathers or use examples from the list below. This bulletin board is similar to "Pop Quiz."

William Faulkner (1897-1962)	Married a widow with two children; they had one child together. Night superintendent of a power plant. Wrote one of his best-known works on an overturned wheelbarrow.
Kenneth Graham (1859-1932)	Wrote *Wind in the Willows* for his one son. Was a banker and a social worker.
Ernest Hemingway (1899-1961)	Had a fishing rod at the age of two and a gun at the age of 10. His father wanted him to be a doctor; his mother wanted him to play the cello.
O. Henry (1862-1910)	Unloaded bananas in New Orleans. Was a bank teller in Austin, Texas. Served three years in the Ohio State Penitentiary.
Langston Hughes (1902-1967)	Was a seaman, a cook, and a busboy. His mother was a teacher.
Aldous Huxley (1894-1963)	Planned to be a doctor, but went completely blind. Learned Braille, though, after two years, one eye improved.
Rudyard Kipling (1865-1936)	Was born in India. Did not attend school until he was 12 years old. Wanted to see the Boer War firsthand.
Sinclair Lewis (1885-1951)	First American to win Noble Prize for literature. Named his son Wells after his friend H. G. Wells. He refused to accept the Pulitzer Prize.
Hugh Lofting (1886-1947)	Attended MIT. Wanted his children to have something to read from him while he served in World War I. Wrote letters and illustrated them with animals that were being used in the war.
Carl Sandburg (1878-1967)	Father changed named from Johnson. He left school at age 13. Was a bricklayer, a dishwasher, and a housepainter.
Siegfried Sassoon (1886-1967)	Fought in World War I. Was wounded and awarded a medal. Threw the medal into the sea, hoping to be court-martialed; instead, he was sent to a mental institution.
Sherwood Anderson (1876-1941)	Each of his brothers and sisters was born in a different town in Ohio. He was married four times.
L. Frank Baum (1856-1919)	Created the characters of Jack Pumpkinhead, Woggle Bug, the Gump, Tik Tok, Woozy, and Teddy Bear, but they did not appear in the film version of his book.
Joseph Conrad (1857-1924)	Almost became a French writer instead of an English one. Born in Russian Poland, he spent most of his young life at sea.
Sir Arthur Conan Doyle (1859-1930)	Received a degree in medicine. Based his most famous character on two of his professors.

READ AND WRITE, AND YOUR GRADES WILL BLOOM

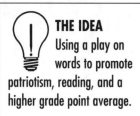

THE IDEA
Using a play on words to promote patriotism, reading, and a higher grade point average.

THE MATERIALS: Cover the board with broad strips of red, white, and blue paper or fabric. The top strip should be red (read); the middle strip, white (write); and the bottom strip, blue (bloom). Write the word "Read" on the red strip, the word "Write" on the white strip, and the phrase "and Your Grades Will Bloom" on the bottom strip. This board could be used during election time (school, local, state, or national elections) or during events such as Flag Day or the Fourth of July.

Cultural Diversity

MULTICULTURAL TITLES ON THE SECONDARY LEVEL

Build a bulletin board around any of these titles or a group of titles to spark appreciation of multiculturalism.

- *Angela's Ashes*/McCourt
- *Love in the Time of Cholera*/Marquez
- *Annie John*/Kincaid
- *Love Medicine*/Erdrich
- *The Bean Trees*/Kingsolver
- *Master Harold and the Boys*/Fugard
- *Bless Me, Ultima*/Anaya
- *Native Son*/Wright
- *The Bluest Eye*/Morrison
- *Picture Bride*/Uchido
- *The Bride Price*/Emecheta
- *Pigs in Heaven*/Kingsolver
- *China Boy*/Lee
- *Seraph on the Suwanee*/Hurston
- *Fences*/Wilson
- *Sula*/Morrison
- *Fool's Crow*/Welch

- *The Rapture of Canaan*/Reynolds
- *A Gathering of Old Men*/Gaines
- *Their Eyes Were Watching God*/Hurston
- *Green Grass, Running Water*/King
- *Things Fall Apart*/Achebe
- *Her Stories*: *A Collection of African-American Tales*/Hamilton
- *Ties That Bind, Ties That Break*/Namioka
- *House on Mango Street*/Cisneros
- *The Tiger's Daughter*/Mukherjee
- *The Hundred Secret Senses*/Tan
- *Waiting for the Rain*/Gordon
- *The Kitchen God's Wife*/Tan
- *Walking Across Egypt*/Edgerton
- *A Lesson Before Dying*/Gaines
- *Your Blues Ain't Like Mine*/Campbell
- *Like Water for Chocolate*/Esquivel

BLACK FACTS

THE IDEA
To promote Black History Month with interesting, but little-known, facts about African Americans.

THE MATERIALS: Cover the board with an African-inspired fabric or with strips of red, black, and green paper or other material. Add the caption "Black Facts" and fascinating information about African Americans. Use material from your library media center or from the examples below:

- Pedro Alonzo Nino was the pilot of the *Santa Maria*, one of Christopher Columbus's ships.
- In 1624, William Tucker was the first black child to born in the land that later became the United States.
- In 1762, James Derham, the first black American physician, was born in Philadelphia.
- One of Paul Revere's Minutemen was Lemuel Hayes, a black patriot.
- Black troops fought in the Battle of New Orleans under General Andrew Jackson in 1814.
- Edward A. Jones was the first black to graduate from college. He received a degree from Amherst College on Aug. 23, 1826. John Russwurm received a degree from Bowdoin College on Sept. 6, 1826.
- *Freedom's Journal* was the first Negro newspaper published in the United States. It was published in 1827 in New York by Russwurm and Samuel E. Cornish.
- *Clotel*, or *The President's Daughter*, written by William Wells Brown, was the first novel published by an African American, in 1853.
- Capital Savings Bank was the first black bank established in the United States, in Washington, D.C., on Oct. 17, 1888.
- Matthew A. Henson was co-discoverer of the North Pole with Robert Peary and four Eskimos. In 1909, he planted the American flag on the spot designated by Peary as the exact location of the Pole.
- In 1787 Richard Allen founded the African Methodist Episcopal Church. This became the first major religious institution for blacks in the United States.
- Prince Hall, one of America's first black civil rights leaders, founded the first Masonic Lodge for black men in 1787.
- John Rock became the first black admitted to practice law before the U.S. Supreme Court in 1865.
- Andrew J. Beard is credited with making an important advance in railroad safety by inventing a coupling device, the Jenny Coupler, for railway cars, in 1896.
- In 1879 Mary Eliza Mohoney was the first African-American woman to graduate as a trained nurse in America. She led the way for the admission of other African-American women to professional nursing. She graduated from the New England Hospital for Women and Children in Boston.
- In 1893 Dr. Daniel Hale performed the first successful heart surgery in America. He was founder of the National Medical Association, an organization of African-American physicians. He also founded Provident Hospital in Chicago, the first U.S. hospital organized by African Americans.
- In 1914 Garrett A. Morgan devised a breathing helmet that enabled rescuers to enter dangerous areas filled with smoke and gas. In 1923, he invented an automatic stop-and-go light, which safely signaled the movement of traffic at street crossings.
- Paul R. Williams was the architect for the city of Los Angeles. He designed many famous hotels, homes, and places of business in southern California.
- The first African-American choreographer for the New York Metropolitan Opera was Katherine Dunham, a spirited dancer who blended African and American dance forms.
- In 1810 the first African-American insurance company, The American Insurance Company of Philadelphia, was established.

BLACK HISTORY TRAILS

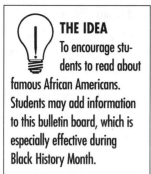

THE IDEA
To encourage students to read about famous African Americans. Students may add information to this bulletin board, which is especially effective during Black History Month.

THE MATERIALS: Place a map of the United States in the center of the bulletin board. As students read about a famous African American, they complete an information card of interesting facts about that person. Students may tell where the person is from, what they did, and why they are remembered. Place red, black, or green ribbon on the map to indicate where the person lived, and put the information card at the end of the ribbon. If many students participate, you may want to change the cards weekly. You may also want to create the information cards and place them on or near the bulletin board.

Idea suggested by Lillian Hairston, Owings Mill (Maryland) High School

BUDDHA'S BIRTHDAY

THE IDEA
To help students learn about the Buddhist faith and its founder, Siddhartha Gautama.

THE MATERIALS: Cover the bulletin board with red fabric or paper. In the center add a cutout of Buddha, and around the cutout, place various facts about "The Enlightened One" and jackets of books about the Buddhist religion. As Buddha's birthday is April 8, 563 B.C.E., April is an appropriate month for this board. Examples of Buddhist facts you may choose to use:

- Siddhartha Gautama was an Indian prince in search of the truth.
- Buddhism has been a dominant religion in most of Asia.
- There are more than 200 million followers of Buddhism.
- In Buddhism, "dharma" has two distinct meanings: It refers to religious truth and it is used as a technical term to signify an element of experience, or any existing thing or phenomenon.
- Buddha believed that existence was a continuous cycle of death and rebirth.
- Buddha believed that people needed to eliminate any attachment to worldly things.
- Nirvana is a state of perfect peace and happiness that people can attain through Buddhism.

DID YOU KNOW?

THE IDEA
To promote Black History Month with important, but little-known, facts.

THE MATERIALS: Cover the bulletin board with strips of red, black, and green paper. The strips can go vertically or horizontally. Add the caption "Did You Know?" in black, followed by interesting facts from your collection or from the suggestions listed below:

- The pilot of the *Santa Maria* was Pedro Alonzo Nino. He was a black man.
- The first man to die in the Boston Massacre, Crispus Attucks, was black.
- The first draft of the Declaration of Independence had a clause that banned slavery.
- Frederick Douglass was an advisor to four presidents.
- Dr. Charles Richard Drew was the developer of the modern blood bank.
- The first black millionaire was Madame C. J. Walker.

You can add book jackets featuring information about African Americans or pictures of people featured in the little-known facts.

EXPERIENCE ASIA

THE IDEA
To encourage students and staff to read about Asian culture and biographies, and expand their knowledge of this part of the world.

THE MATERIALS: You could use the flags of several Asian countries as a background for this board. (You may want to check with the school counselors to see what Asian nations are represented in your school and create the flags of those nations.) If time is an issue, cover the board with colorful fabric or paper and add the caption "Experience Asia." Use book jackets from your collection of Asian leaders, countries, and cultures.
Some examples of people you may choose to spotlight are:

East Asia	South Asia	Southeast Asia	Central Asia
Zhou Enlai	Subhas Chandra Bose	Bhumibol Adulyadej	Ayatollah Khomeini
Hirohito	Mohammad Ali Jinnah	Damrong Rajanubhab	Mohammed Mossadegh
Chiang Kai-shek	Mohammad Ayub Khan	Ho Chi Minh	
Kim Dae Jung	Indira Gandhi	Aung San	
Kim Il Sung	Mohandas Gandhi	Sukarno	
Kim Jong Il	Jawaharlal Nehru		
Chang Myon	Dalai Lama		
Syngman Rhee			
Mao Zedong			

HAPPY NEW YEAR AROUND THE GLOBE

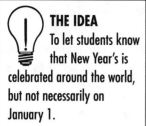

THE IDEA
To let students know that New Year's is celebrated around the world, but not necessarily on January 1.

THE MATERIALS: Cover your January board with colorful paper or fabric. Place noisemakers or party hats around the caption "Happy New Year Around the Globe." Add New Year greetings and information about customs from other nations. You may want to focus on a variety of countries or concentrate on those countries that represent your student population. For instance, you could spotlight:

■ China: New Year's Eve is called Wahn Than and is celebrated with a dinner of fish, eggs, pork, and vegetables. New Year's is also a birthday celebration, and children receive monetary gifts from their relatives. People wish each other "Kung Hi" ("I wish you joy!").

■ Japan: New Year's Eve is called Osho Gatsu. Most people take several days off in order to celebrate. Homes are decorated with bamboo and berries that symbolize long life and happiness.

■ Spain: In Spain, and some Spanish-speaking countries, people celebrate New Year's Eve by having 12 grapes ready to eat when the clock starts to chime midnight. (It is traditional to listen to the clock from Puerta del Sol in Madrid.) At midnight, each time the clock chimes, the celebrants put a grape in their mouth. By the time the clock has finished chiming, everybody is supposed to have finished their grapes, and the New Year officially starts (but nobody finishes eating the grapes on time).

■ Mexico: In Mexico, many people gather with their relatives and friends to celebrate the New Year. Like in Spain, at midnight, each time a bell rings, they eat one grape and make a wish. Then they hug each other and wish each other a Happy New Year. Some people, especially women, wear red underwear, which means they hope to find love in the next year. Some people take out their suitcases and walk around the block, which means they want to travel in the next year.

■ Thailand: The Thai New Year is celebrated on April 13. This is also the day of a special festival called Song-Klarn Day. On this day, Thai people play with water, throwing it on each other. This Thai holiday also focuses on respecting senior citizens, so most Thai people go back to their hometowns to visit their grandparents and ask them for good luck. On the morning of January 1, children often ask for blessings or good wishes from their parents and grandparents, and both sets of elders give the children money. Some families have fireworks, too.

■ Vietnam: New Year's is celebrated over a three-day period in this country. On the first day, at midnight, the grandmother or mother of each family lights firecrackers to receive and welcome the New Year. Then, the family goes to sleep to wait for the sunrise. When the sun rises, the Vietnamese people wake up and put on new clothes. Then, grandparents sit on chairs in front of their children to wish them a Happy New Year and a long life. Then, parents sit on the chairs to wish their children the same thing.

HISPANIC HISTORY

THE IDEA
To promote the contributions and accomplishments of both Hispanic Americans and Hispanics of other countries. This is a great bulletin board for Cultural Diversity Month or Hispanic Culture Month, or just to salute famous Hispanics who have had an impact on history, entertainment, sports, or politics.

THE MATERIALS: Cover the bulletin board with yellow paper. Include pictures of famous Hispanics and Hispanic Americans. Use the sample list of Web sites below or create your own list. Remember to check the sites regularly to see if they are still active and appropriate for your needs.

- America USA Table of Contents <www.neta.com/~1stbooks/content.htm>
- Biographies <www.ecnet.net/users/gdlevin/myreferencepoints/biographies.htm>
- Biography.com <www.biography.com>
- Californio Biographies <www.sandiegohistory.org/bio/californios.htm>
- Cesar Chavez <www.incwell.com/Biographies/Chavez.html>
- Cesar Chavez Biography <www.mit.edu/afs/athena.mit.edu/course/21/21f704/Chicano/Cesar_Chavez_Biography.html>
- Famous Hispanics <coloquio.com/famosos/alpha.html>
- Famous Hispanics <starnet.esc20.k12.tx.us/elem-spanish/famous.htm>
- Famous Hispanics—Writers and Artists <www.snybuf.edu/~spanish/famous.htm>
- Gary Soto
- Hispanic Americans <www.rbls.lib.il.us/dpl/hispanic.htm>
- Hispanic Americans <americanhistory.about.com/homework/americanhistory/msub15.htm>
- Hispanic History <edWeb.sdsu.edu/SDHS/links/hispanicmonth.htm>
- HISPANIC Online on the Web <www.hisp.com/index.html>
- Hispanos Famosos <coloquio.com/famosos.html>
- Joan Baez <hallmall.com/cgi-bin/redirect/go2.cgi?search=JoanBaez&site=BIOGRAPHY>
- Latin American <www.lanexus.com/posters-bios.html>
- Latino Legends in Sports Archives <www.latinosportslegends.com/archives.htm>
- Latino/Hispanic Resources <www.tenet.edu/latino/latino.html>
- Latinos <www.flushing.k12.mi.us/fjh/gill/Latinos.html>
- Linda Ronstadt <disney.go.com/DisneyRecords/Biographies/Ronstadt_Bio.html>
- Mexican History <www.mexonline.com/history.htm>
- People <educate.si.edu/scitech/impacto/graphic/people.html>
- Rita Moreno <www.geocities.com/Hollywood/9766/moreno.html>
- San Diego Biographies <www.sandiegohistory.org/bio/biographies.htm>
- SPI Hispanic Web <www.uky.edu/ArtsSciences/SPI/SPILAWeb.html>
- United States of American History <www.neta.com/~1st books/>
- Villasenor Biography <www.victorvillasenor.com/bio.html>

I LOVE YOU

THE IDEA
For February or for a multicultural celebration, put some of these words of love on your bulletin board.

THE MATERIALS: Cover your bulletin board with white or pink paper. Write the words below, which read "I love you" in different languages, on red hearts. You may want to use languages with which your students are familiar or languages spoken in your school, or to expose the students to a wide variety of foreign languages, such as:

- Afrikaans: Ek is lief vir jou
- Apache: Sheth she~n zho~n
- Armenian: Yes kez si'rumem
- Bangladesch: Ami tomake walobashi
- Bosnian: Volim te
- Brazilian/Portuguese: Eu te amo/Galician: Querote
- Bulgarian: Obicham te
- Burmese: Chit pa de
- Cajun: Mi aime jou
- Cambodian: Kh_nhaum soro_lahn nhee_ah
- Canadian French: Je t'adore
- Cherokee: Aya gvgeyu'i nihi
- Cheyenne: Ne mohotatse
- Chichewa: Ndimakukonda
- Chickasaw: Chiholloli
- Chinese: Gwa ai li
- Croatian: Ja te volim
- Czech: Miluji te
- Danish: Jeg elsker dig
- Dutch: Ik hou van je
- English: I love you
- Estonian: Mina armastan sind
- Ethiopian: Afgreki'
- Farsi: Tora dost daram
- Filipino: Iniibig kita
- French: Je t'aime

- Gaelic: Ta gra agam ort
- Greek: S'ayapo
- Hawaiian: Aloha wau ia 'oe
- Hebrew: Anee ohev otakh
- Hindi: Mai tumase pyar karata hun
- Hungarian: Szeretlek
- Indonesia: Saya cinta padamu
- Italian: Ti amo
- Irish: Taim i'ngra leat
- Japanese: Kimi o aishiteiru
- Korea: (Tangsinul) Saranghae
- Lao: Khoi hak jao
- Latin: Te amo
- Lebanese: Bahibak
- Polish: Kocham cie
- Portuguese: Eu amo-te
- Romanian: Te iubesc
- Russian: Ya tyebya lyublyu
- Spanish: Te amo
- Swahili: Nakupenda
- Swedish: Jag a"lskar dig
- Syrian/Lebanese: Bhebbek
- Thai: Khao raak thoe
- Turkish: Seni seviyorum
- Ukrainian: Ya tebe kokhayu
- Vietnamese: Toi yeu em
- Yugoslavian: Ja te volim

LIVIN' LA VIDA (HIGH SCHOOL)

THE IDEA
Insert your school's name into the title of the Ricky Martin hit to spotlight your school and/or books on Hispanic culture. (We actually used this as our Homecoming theme one year, and the students loved it.)

THE MATERIALS: Cover the bulletin board with one of your school's colors. Add the caption "Livin' La Vida (your school name)" in another school color. You can add pictures and photographs of your students or jackets of books about Hispanic culture, countries, and customs.

MARTIN LUTHER KING JR.

THE IDEA
To promote Black History Month and to inform students about various aspects of Martin Luther King's life.

THE MATERIALS: Cover the board with suitably colored paper. Add the caption "Did you know this about Martin Luther King Jr.?" A drawing or photograph of Rev. King should be placed in the center of the board. Around the photo, place jackets of appropriate books from your collection, as well as interesting facts about this Noble Prize-winner's life, such as:

- Martin Luther King was named "Michael" when he was born.
- Because he dressed so well as a young man, Martin Luther King's nickname was "Tweed."
- Martin Luther King Jr. attended Morehouse College in Atlanta, Georgia.
- Martin Luther King was *Time* Magazine's Man of the Year in 1964. His picture was on the cover of the same magazine in 1957.
- He was the first African American chosen as *Time* Magazine's Man of the Year.
- Martin Luther King's father wanted him to enter the ministry, but Rev. King wanted to study medicine or law.
- Martin Luther King was sentenced to four months hard labor for a traffic violation.
- Dr. Martin Luther King met with Richard Nixon, Dwight Eisenhower, John Kennedy, and Lyndon Johnson.
- He met Malcolm X only once.
- The Martin Luther King holiday was first observed in 1986. It had been proposed 18 years earlier.
- Martin Luther King's first book was *Stride Toward Freedom*. He was 29 years old when it was published.
- Dr. King was the youngest person to receive the Nobel Peace Prize, at the age of 35.

OUR SCHOOL IS ONE SCHOOL

THE IDEA
To celebrate all of the diverse cultures represented in your school.

THE MATERIALS: Cover the bulletin board with your school colors. Using several sheets of poster board or construction paper, draw one letter on each sheet to spell the name of your school. Ask a few members of each culture or group represented in your school to hold one of the letters. You may have African-Americans, Asians, Caucasians, Hispanics, and others. You may also want to include faculty members and the janitorial staff. Take a picture of each group and place it on the bulletin board with a + (plus) sign between each picture. Your board will spell out the name of your school, e.g., "L+O+V+E+J+O+Y = one school."

To generate student involvement, send a notice to selected students that reads:

Dear Student,

This is your special invitation to be famous! I am taking a picture of students from all the cultures represented in our school. I would like to take your picture and place it on the media center bulletin board. Please come to the media center on (date). This note will serve as your pass. The picture will be on the bulletin board during the month of April. Have questions? Please ask. Thanks.

RAMADAN, CHANUKAH, CHRISTMAS, AND KWANZAA

THE IDEA
To inform students and staff about the four major holidays that occur during the winter.

THE MATERIALS: Cover the board with colorful fabric or paper. Add the caption "Ramadan, Chanukah, Christmas, and Kwanzaa." Each word should be in a different color, to distinguish among the four holidays. Information about each holiday, such as the information below, should be listed below each word.

Ramadan: The Muslim holiday lasts about a month. It is the holy month of fasting. The appearance of the crescent moon is the traditional beginning of the Ramadan month. Muslims who keep Ramadan cannot eat during the day for the entire month. The holiday ends in a three-day festival. (Note: Ramadan does not always occur during the winter months.)

Chanukah: The Jewish Feast of Lights begins at sunset on a different day each year, so check your calendar for the exact day. The word "Chanukah" or "Hanukkah" means "dedication." The holiday lasts for eight days, during which gifts are exchanged and contributions are given to the poor. Each night a candle is lighted in the menorah.

Christmas: Christmas celebrates the birth of Jesus Christ, and Christians celebrate the holiday throughout the world. Most people celebrate Christmas on December 25, by exchanging presents and attending church. Homes are decorated with Christmas trees, mistletoe, and holly.

Kwanzaa: Many African Americans celebrate Kwanzaa, which is held December 26 through January 1. Maulana Karenga, a Professor at California State University, began it in 1966. There are seven principles of Kwanzaa: Umoja (unity), Kujichagulia (self-determination), Ujima (collective work and responsibility), Ujama (cooperative economics), Nia (purpose), Kuumba (creativity), and Imani (faith).

SI YOUR LIBRARY MEDIA CENTER!

THE IDEA
To promote your materials on Spanish-speaking countries and items in your collection that are written in Spanish.

THE MATERIALS: Cover your bulletin board with red fabric or paper. Add the caption "Si Your Library Media Center!" in bright yellow. Add jackets of books about Spanish-speaking countries and Hispanic biographies, or of books written in Spanish.

THANK YOU, CARTER G. WOODSON

THE IDEA
To promote Black History Month using the name of the person who originated the celebration.

THE MATERIALS: Cover the board with strips of black, red, and green paper. Add the caption "Thank You, Carter G. Woodson" in a contrasting color. Or, cover the board in black paper or fabric and write the caption in alternating colors of red, green, and black. Add the sample quotes by Woodson listed below or find ones that you feel are appropriate. Add pictures of famous African Americans and interesting facts about Black History Month.

Quotes by Carter G. Woodson:

"Truth must be dug up from the past and presented to the circle of scholastics in scientific form and then through stories and dramatizations that will permeate our educational system."

"Truth comes to us from the past, then, like gold washed down from the mountains."

"The educational system of a country is worthless unless it revolutionizes the social order. Men of scholarship, and prophetic insight, must show us the right way and lead us into light which is shining brighter and brighter."

"We need workers, not leaders. Such workers will solve the problems which race leaders talk about."

"In the long run, there is not much discrimination against superior talent. It constrains men to recognize it."

WE ARE A KALEIDOSCOPE OF CULTURES

THE IDEA
To introduce students and staff to the different cultures represented in your school.

THE MATERIALS: Cover the board in neutral fabric or paper. Using different colors of paper for each letter, add the caption "We Are a Kaleidoscope of Cultures." Use pictures or photographs of groups of students to illustrate your school's diversity. Add book jackets that represent authors from the students' countries or culture, or jackets from travel books about that part of the world.

WE ARE DIFFERENT, WE ARE THE SAME

THE IDEA
To promote and celebrate your school's cultural differences and similarities.

THE MATERIALS: Cover the board with colorful fabric, perhaps strips of black, white, red, yellow, and brown. Add the caption "We Are Different, We Are the Same." If you choose a solid background for the bulletin board, you may want to cut the letters out of different colors. Add book jackets from biographies, historical titles, and books about the accomplishments of people of different ethnic backgrounds. For extra interest add a nonbreakable mirror to the middle of the board.

UNDERSTANDING ISLAM

THE IDEA
To provide basic knowledge of the Islamic faith by explaining the Five Pillars of Islam.

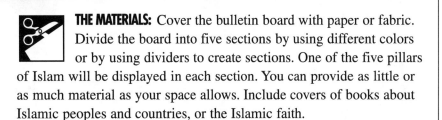

THE MATERIALS: Cover the bulletin board with paper or fabric. Divide the board into five sections by using different colors or by using dividers to create sections. One of the five pillars of Islam will be displayed in each section. You can provide as little or as much material as your space allows. Include covers of books about Islamic peoples and countries, or the Islamic faith.

The Five Pillars:
1) *Faith*: There is no god worthy of worship except God, and Muhammad is His messenger. This declaration of faith is called the Shahada.
2) *Prayer*: Salat is the name for the obligatory prayers that are performed five times a day and are a direct link between the worshipper and God. There is no hierarchical authority in Islam, and no priests, so the prayers are led by a learned person, chosen by the congregation, who knows the Qur'an.
3) *The Zakat* (purification and growth): One of the most important principles of Islam is that all things belong to God, and that wealth is therefore held by human beings in trust.
4) *The Fast*: Every year in the month of Ramadan, all Muslims fast from first light until sundown, abstaining from food and drink.
5) *The Pilgrimage*: The annual pilgrimage to Makkah (Mecca) is an obligation only for those who are physically and financially able to perform it. Nevertheless, about two million people go to Makkah each year, from every corner of the globe, providing a unique opportunity for those of different nations to meet one another.

The Bookstore

BET YOU CAN'T READ JUST ONE!

THE IDEA
To promote sequels or books in a series.

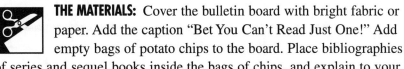

THE MATERIALS: Cover the bulletin board with bright fabric or paper. Add the caption "Bet You Can't Read Just One!" Add empty bags of potato chips to the board. Place bibliographies of series and sequel books inside the bags of chips, and explain to your patrons that the lists on the bulletin board are for students' use.

(Remind students to return the lists to the chip bags when they have found the book they want.)

See appendix for an example of this bulletin board. (Chart L)

Idea suggested by Linda Locker, Harmon Middle School, Pickerington, Ohio

THE IDEA
To test students' and faculty's knowledge of literature. List the original titles of famous works and see if they can determine the actual title.

THE MATERIALS: Cover the board with colorful paper. Add the caption "Can you match these original titles of famous books with their actual title?" You can use examples from the list below or create a list of your own. This becomes a matching game when students and faculty try to determine which title goes with which. You may ask patrons to use research skills to determine the right answer, or you may want to just list the titles as suggestions for interesting reading. Include the book jackets of some of the titles mentioned.

ample list:

ORIGINAL TITLE	ACTUAL TITLE
Catch-18	*Catch-22*
Mag's Diversions	*David Copperfield*
Terror of the Monster	*Jaws*
The Chronic Argonauts	*The Time Machine*
Ba! Ba! Black Sheep	*Gone with the Wind*
The Sea Cook	*Treasure Island*
Before This Anger	*Roots*
Salinas Valley	*East of Eden*
Something That Happened	*Of Mice and Men*
Fiesta	*The Sun Also Rises*
All's Well That Ends Well	*War and Peace*
The Village Virus	*Main Street*

C D B

THE IDEA
Using William Steig's adorable book *C D B* as inspiration, create a bulletin board with just letters. Student suggestions and ideas can be added to the board during the weeks it is on display. You will probably want to read the book to the students or have it on display so that the students "get" the connection.

THE MATERIALS: Cover the board with colorful fabric or paper. In large letters add the caption "C D B." Add a couple of young people and a bumblebee. Additional puzzle letters can be added with a request that students try their hand at writing a similar sentence.

Suggestions for puzzle sentences:

I C U. (I see you.)

I 8 U. (I hate you.)

I N-V U. (I envy you.)

S M-T. (It's empty.)

HARRY POTTER GOES TO HIGH SCHOOL

THE IDEA This bulletin board takes advantage of the *Harry Potter* craze—high school students and even adults are reading this series. If your library does not own any copies of these books, or if it does, but they are continually checked out, this board encourages your patrons to try similar books.

THE MATERIALS: Cover the board with yellow paper and write the caption "*Harry Potter* Goes to High School" in red. Place a picture of Harry in the center; Harry with a mortarboard on his head would be especially appealing to high school students. Add book jackets or digital pictures of books from the same genre. For instance, titles by authors such as Tolkein, Dahl, LeGuin, Alexander, Susan Cooper, and Jane Yolen are similar to the *Harry Potter* books. A banner at the bottom of the bulletin board can read, "Checkout these titles."

See appendix for an example of this bulletin board. (Chart E)

HAVEN'T GOT A CLUE? CHECK OUT THESE MYSTERIES

THE IDEA To promote mystery and detective books. Some patrons have never attempted to read a mystery novel, but might enjoy tales by Lois Duncan, Agatha Christie, Sue Grafton, Ian Fleming, Stephen Coonts, Patricia Cornwell, or many other mystery writers.

THE MATERIALS: Cover the bulletin board with black paper or fabric. Draw a huge magnifying glass in a corner of the board. Add the caption "Haven't Got a Clue?" Place authors' names and book jackets on the board. Use the names of the authors suggested to the left or use the names of authors from your collection. At the bottom of the board add, "Checkout These Mysteries."

LET'S GET PERSONAL

THE IDEA To promote biographies and auto-biographies.

THE MATERIALS: Cover your bulletin board with the classified section of your newspaper. Add the caption "Let's Get Personal" in black letters. Create small "personal ads" about various people represented in your biography section and place the ads on the background. For example, the "ad" for a biography on Thomas Jefferson may read:

I have red hair, great writing ability, and beautiful penmanship. I helped to double the size of the United States and I planned the city of Washington, D.C. I can be reached in the Biography section. My address is Bio/Jef.

Use biographies from your library media center. Students may want to create some of the ads. See appendix for an example of this bulletin board. (Chart F)

THE IDEA
To whet students' appetites for quality literature with titles that mention food or meals.

THE MATERIALS: Cover the board with a tablecloth-type material or colorful paper. Add the caption "A Literary Feast." If you choose to use paper as the background, add some paper plates and plastic spoons and forks for a touch of flavor. You can use your own titles or choose from the list below:

- *The Chocolate War*/Cormier
- *The Bean Trees*/Kingsolver
- *Who Moved My Cheese?*/Johnson
- *Dinner at the Homesick Café*/Tyler
- *Teacup Full of Roses*/Mathis
- *The Cider House Rules*/Irving

- *The House on Mango Street*/Cisneros
- *The Kitchen God's Wife*/Tan
- *Like Water for Chocolate*/Esquivel
- *Ballad of the Sad Café*/McCullers
- *The Tragedy of Puddin'head Wilson*/Twain
- *Chicken Soup for the Teenage Soul*/Canfield

A REAL TASTE FOR LITERATURE

THE IDEA
Similar to "A Literary Feast," this board uses titles that mention food to encourage your patrons to read.

THE MATERIALS: Use a picnic tablecloth as the background. Place paper plates on the tablecloth and a copy of a book jacket on each plate. Add interest by including picnic items such as a bottle of ketchup, bowls of chips, and maybe even a few ants marching across the board. Use some of the titles listed below or create your own menu of titles:

- *The Chocolate War*/ Cormier
- *The Bean Trees*/ Kingsolver
- *The Cherry Orchard*/ Mamet
- *Dinner at the Homesick Café*/ Tyler
- *Teacup Full of Roses*/ Mathis
- *The Cider House Rules*/Irving

- *The House on Mango Street*/ Cisneros
- *The Kitchen God's Wife*/ Tan
- *Like Water for Chocolate*/ Esquivel
- *Ballad of the Sad Café*/ McCullers
- *The Tragedy of Puddin'head Wilson*/ Twain
- *The Grapes of Wrath*/Steinbeck

MUCH ADO ABOUT BOOKS

THE IDEA This play on words is a springboard to a Shakespearean bulletin board. Media specialists/librarians can use this catchy phrase to showcase Shakespearean plays and poetry.

THE MATERIALS: With "Much Ado about Books" as the caption, add book jackets or digital pictures of Shakespearean books. Add quotes from William Shakespeare and pictures of The Globe Theatre.

Idea suggested by the Jacksonville (Florida) Public Library system

OUR RAINBOW HAS A REAL POT OF GOLD AT THE END

THE IDEA In folklore there is an imaginary pot of gold at the end of the rainbow, but at the end of this library rainbow there is a real container of education and knowledge.

THE MATERIALS: Cover the board with blue paper or material. Create a colorful rainbow with strips of paper. On each strip write a title that corresponds to that color. For example, on the red strip write *The Scarlet Letter* or *The Red Badge of Courage*. On the purple strip write *The Color Purple*. On a black strip write *Black Like Me*. Draw a leprechaun's pot and place it at the end of the rainbow. Write the words "education" and "knowledge" so that they are emerging from the pot.

READ THE FINE PRINT

THE IDEA To encourage students to use the indices of encyclopedias, atlases, and other reference and nonfiction books. Students often do not use a book's index, but either head straight for the Table of Contents or expect the information to just appear before them. The index is a vital part of the reference search, and it is where the student can find valuable information.

THE MATERIALS: Use the caption "Read the Fine Print." To really grab students' attention, however, make the lettering as small as possible while keeping it legible. Attach index pages from material in your library media center to the board. On the index pages, highlight recent topics for which students have searched to emphasize the value of using the index.

REEL ALTERNATIVES

THE IDEA
To promote books that have been made into movies.

THE MATERIALS: Cover the bulletin board with black fabric or paper. Instead of a border, add fabric or paper curtains that have been pulled back at either side of the board. Add the caption "Reel Alternatives" and list the titles of book that have been made into movies. Use titles from your own collection or from the examples listed below. (See "Don't Judge a Book by Its Movie" below for more examples.)

- *To Kill a Mockingbird*/Lee
- *The Wizard of Oz*/Baum
- *Bridge Over the River Kwai*/Boulle
- *Gone With the Wind*/Mitchell
- *Rebecca*/DuMaurier
- *The Grapes of Wrath*/Steinbeck
- *A Streetcar Named Desire*/Williams
- *All Quiet on the Western Front*/Remarque
- *Henry V*/Shakespeare

- *All the President's Men*/Bernstein
- *The 39 Steps*/Christie
- *Ordinary People*/Guest
- *One Flew over the Cuckoo's Nest*/Kesey
- *All the King's Men*/Warren
- *Sense and Sensibility*/Austen
- *The Taming of the Shrew*/Shakespeare
- *Catch-22*/Heller
- *Pride and Prejudice*/Austen
- *Out of Africa*/Dinesen

See appendix for an example of this bulletin board. (Chart R)

YOU CAN'T JUDGE A BOOK BY ITS MOVIE

THE IDEA
As with "Reel Alternatives," to promote the reading of books that have been made into feature films.

THE MATERIALS: Cover your bulletin board with black paper. Add the caption "You can't judge a book by its movie" and place bright yellow stars around the border. Using books from your collection, find titles that have been made into films and attach the jackets to the board. Students will be surprised to discover that some of their favorite movies were first books. Filmmakers often leave important details out of their version of a story, due to time constraints and the inability to transfer a scene from paper to film. Understanding this may encourage your patrons to see what was missing from their favorite movie. Try the following titles:

- *Jurassic Park*/Crichton
- *Alias Madame Doubtfire*/Fine
- *Cold Sassy Tree*/Burns
- *The Hunt for Red October*/Clancy
- *Beloved*/Morrison

- *The Outsiders*/Hinton
- *Tex*/Hinton
- *Forrest Gump*/Groom
- *2001: A Space Odyssey*/Clarke

SECRETS AND LIES

 THE IDEA
To promote books that deal with betrayal, twists of fate, secrets, and deception.

 THE MATERIALS: Cover the bulletin board with black paper. Add the caption "Secrets and Lies." Post titles of books that explore deception, secrets, and falsehoods. Use titles from the list below or develop a list from your collection.

- *Othello*/Shakespeare
- *The Icarus Agenda*/Ludlum
- *Jane Eyre*/Bronte
- *The Picture of Dorian Gray*/Wilde
- *The House of Dies Drear*/Hamilton

- *Dr. Jekyll and Mr. Hyde*/Stevenson
- *Summer of My German Soldier*/Greene
- *All the King's Men*/Warren
- *The Game of the Foxes*/Farago
- *The Thirty-Nine Steps*/Buchan
- *Rebecca*/DuMaurier

SPECIAL DELIVERY

 THE IDEA
To promote collections of letters, either real or imagined.

 THE MATERIALS: Cover the bulletin board with white paper so that it resembles an envelope and attach a "stamp" in the upper-right corner. Add the caption "Special Delivery." Post titles of books from the list below or find books in your collection that compile letters written to actual or imaginary people.

- *The Screwtape Letters*/Lewis
- *I Love You, Ronnie*/Reagan
- *Letters from Pemberley, the First Year: A Continuation of Jane Austen's Pride and Prejudice*/Dawkins
- *The Greatest Generation Speaks: Letters and Reflections*/Brokaw
- *All the Best, George Bush: My Life in Letters and Other Writings*/Bush
- *Hour of Gold, Hour of Lead: Diaries and Letters of Anne Morrow Lindbergh 1929-1932*/Lindbergh
- *Letters from the Earth*/Twain
- *Birthday Letters*/Hughes
- *Thomas Paine: Pamphlets, Articles and Letters*/Paine
- *Letters from the Inside*/Marsden

THROUGH THE YEAR WITH BOOKS

THE IDEA
To encourage reading throughout the year by spotlighting titles or authors whose names are associated with the calendar.

THE MATERIALS: Cover the board with colorful paper. Add the caption "Through the Year with Books." Divide a large piece of paper into 12 squares to create a calendar. Label each square with a month of the year. In each square place a title or a book jacket that corresponds with that month. Use the list below or create your own:

January: *Night of January 16th*/Rand

February: *A History of Russia*/Riasanovsky

March: *The Adventures of Augie March*/Bellow

April: *April Morning*/Fast, or *April 1865*/Winik

May: *Little Women*/Alcott

June: *The Longest Day: June 6, 1944*/Ryan

July: *Born on the 4th of July*/Kovic

August: *Fences*/Wilson

September: *Miracle at Philadelphia: The Story of the Constitutional Convention, May to September 1787*/Bowen

October: *The Hunt for Red October*/Clancy

November: *The Gates of November: Chronicles of the Slepak Family*/Potok

December*: Air Raid—Pearl Harbor!: The Story of December 7, 1941*/Taylor

See appendix for an example of this bulletin board. (Chart G)
Idea suggested by Maggie Serritella, student, State University of West Georgia

WANT TO READ ABOUT REAL-LIFE SURVIVORS? TRY THESE

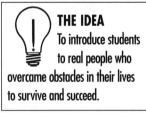

THE IDEA
To introduce students to real people who overcame obstacles in their lives to survive and succeed.

THE MATERIALS: Cover the board with blue paper. Add the caption "Want to read about real survivors? Try these." Cutouts of an island with a palm tree and a bright orange sun in one corner will give the board a tropical feel. Add these titles or choose some of your own:

- *Into Thin Air*/Krakauer
- *The Climb*/Boukreev
- *Paddle to the Amazon*/Starkell
- *Alive*/Read
- *Kon Tiki*/Heyerdahl
- *Z for Zachariah*/O'Brien
- *The Cay*/Taylor
- *Robinson Crusoe*/Defoe (Based on the true story of Alexander Selkirk)

WHAT'S COOKIN' IN THE MEDIA CENTER?

THE IDEA
Increase your patrons' appetite for good literature by featuring titles that mention food.

THE MATERIALS: Cover the bulletin board with colorful paper. Add the caption "What's cookin' in the media center?" Cut a large pot and a chef from construction paper and place them in the center of the board. Post the titles listed below or think of other titles that mention cuisine or cooking:

- *The Grapes of Wrath*/Steinbeck
- *Catcher in the Rye*/Salinger
- *Breakfast at Tiffany's*/Capote
- *Like Chocolate for Water*/Esquivel
- *The Adventures of Huckleberry Finn*/Twain
- *New Grub Street*/Gissing
- *Burger's Daughter*/Gordimer
- *A Clockwork Orange*/Burgess
- *The Count of Monte Cristo*/Dumas
- *The Naked Lunch*/Burroughs
- *Chicken Soup for the Teenage Soul*/Canfield

SOCIAL LOSERS

THE IDEA
To promote biographies or nonfiction books about people who were wicked or corrupt. (This board may not be to everyone's liking, but students are always asking for books in this genre.)

THE MATERIALS: Cover the bulletin board with black paper. Add the caption "Social Losers." Scatter around the board paper drawings of books with evil-looking faces on them. Use the books mentioned below or books from your collection that fit the criteria.

Use books about Adolf Hitler, Pol Pot, Bonnie and Clyde, John Dillinger, Mata Hari, Charles Manson, Jack the Ripper, Al Capone, Lizzie Borden, Jesse James, gun violence, juvenile crime, gangsters, or criminals.

Author!
Author!

ARTHUR! ARTHUR!

THE IDEA
To promote authors whose first, middle, or last name is Arthur. Several authors fit this category, and you can promote both the authors and their writing by featuring them with this play on words.

THE MATERIALS: Cover the board with colorful paper or fabric. Cut out letters to spell "Arthur! Arthur!" Around the caption, arrange jackets of the authors' books and/or pictures of the featured writers. Some Arthur's you may want to include are Sir Arthur Conan Doyle, Arthur Miller, Arthur Clarke, Arthur Schlesinger Jr., Eric Arthur Blair, Arthur Rackham, and Arthur Hailey.

I CAN SEE CLEARY, NOW

THE IDEA
Although some secondary students may think they are too mature for Beverly Cleary's books, she remains a popular author for all ages. A play on her name and the song "I Can See Clearly, Now" should grab students' attention.

THE MATERIALS: The caption "I Can See Cleary, Now" should be at the top of the board, with a picture or photograph of Cleary in the center. Include several titles of her books, or book jackets, around her photograph. Ask students to tell you about their favorite Cleary book and add that information. You may want to take pictures of students reading Cleary's titles.

BILL OF WRITES

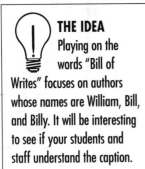

THE IDEA
Playing on the words "Bill of Writes" focuses on authors whose names are William, Bill, and Billy. It will be interesting to see if your students and staff understand the caption.

THE MATERIALS: Cover the board with colorful paper or fabric. Add the caption "Bill of Writes." Attach jackets of books by writers with "Bill," "Billy," "William," or "Williams" in their name. Use names from the list below or create your own:

- William Faulkner
- William Golding
- William Shakespeare
- William Sleator
- Tennessee Williams

See appendix for an example of this bulletin board. (Chart N)

BLUME AND GROW

THE IDEA
To promote books written by Judy Blume.

THE MATERIALS: Cover the bulletin board with green paper or fabric. Add the caption "Blume and Grow." Attach paper flowers at the base of the bulletin board. Inside the flowers, place a picture of Blume and titles of her books that would appeal to your students.

BY GEORGE!

THE IDEA
To promote books written by authors with George in their name.

THE MATERIALS: Cover the bulletin board with colorful paper or fabric. Add the caption "By George!" in a coordinating color. Add pictures of authors and jackets of books by people who have "George" in their name. Use titles from your collection or the examples listed below:

- George Eliot
- George Bernard Shaw
- H. G. Wells (Herbert George)
- Jean Craighead George
- George Orwell
- Elizabeth George Speare
- George Gordon, Lord Byron

See appendix for an example of this bulletin board. (Chart B)

CHECKOUT OUR HOMEGROWN CROP

THE IDEA
To feature authors or illustrators from your geographical area. You may concentrate on your town, the entire state, or the larger region in which you live. Students and faculty may not be aware of the close proximity of writers with whom they may be familiar.

THE MATERIALS: Cover the bulletin board with colorful material or paper. Place a map of your area in the center of the board. Add the caption "Checkout Our Homegrown Crop." Position pictures of local writers or their books' jackets around the map. Draw an arrow from the picture of the author to the city or town on the map where the author lives.

CHILDHOOD REMINISCENCES

THE IDEA
To promote the art department, inspire students, and introduce students to author and artist Faith Ringgold.

THE MATERIALS: Obtain 12 x 12 squares of poster board and cut scraps of calico material into two-inch squares. Have students in the art classes draw pictures of a favorite memory from their childhood. The pictures need to be colorful and accompanied by a brief (two or three sentences) statement about what the drawing represents. After the artwork is complete, use the squares of calico to piece together a border around the artwork. (The calico can be glued to the poster board.) Arrange the squares on the bulletin board so that it resembles a quilt. Place materials about Ringgold next to the board for students and staff to check out.

Idea suggested by Sandra Sparks, Morrow (Georgia) High School

GOT SIX WEEKS TO SPARE? WRITE A BOOK

THE IDEA Many students dread the thought of writing a theme or research paper, let alone an entire book. This list of authors who wrote entire novels in less than six weeks may inspire them.

THE MATERIALS: Cover your bulletin board with white paper and trim it with a black border (or reverse the colors). Add the caption "Got six weeks to spare? Write a book." Create your own list of authors or use the list below to show students that writing a brilliant tome or best-seller does not necessarily imply years and years spent hammering away at the keyboard.

AUTHOR	TITLE	LENGTH OF TIME IT TOOK TO COMPLETE THE BOOK
Louisa May Alcott	*Little Men*	3 weeks
Honore de Balzac	*Le Pere Goriot*	1 month, 10 days
Daniel Defoe	*Further Adventures of Robinson Crusoe*	1 month
Erle Stanley Gardner	*Case of the Velvet Claws*	3 days
James Hilton	*Goodbye, Mr. Chips*	4 days
Anne Rice	*Interview with a Vampire*	5 weeks
Robert Louis Stevenson	*Strange Case of Dr. Jekyll and Mr. Hyde*	3 days

SHAKESPEARE, EMERSON, MORRISON... NEED WE SAY MORE?

THE IDEA To promote well-known authors in a succinct way.

THE MATERIALS: Cover the bulletin board with a colorful paper and add the caption "Shakespeare, Emerson, Morrison... need we say more?" You can change the names of the authors to appeal to your students. Add pictures of the authors and their books' jackets.

TAKE THIS POP QUIZ (FAMOUS DADS)

 **THE IDEA** To promote famous writers who were also fathers.

 THE MATERIALS: Cover the bulletin board with a dark fabric or paper. Add the caption "Take This Pop Quiz." This bulletin board works at any time during the year, but is especially useful around Father's Day.

Sample quiz:

1. This pop was tall, athletic, and a better-than-average golfer. His son, Christopher Robin, also became an author. Answer: A. A. Milne (1882-1956)

2. This dad was born in Savannah, Georgia. He became the first American poet to be excused from war duty in order to write poetry. Answer: Conrad Aiken (1889-1973)

3. This pop had six brothers and sisters. Each one was born in a different town in Ohio. He was married four times and had two sons and one daughter. Answer: Sherwood Anderson (1876-1941)

4. This father created characters Jack Pumpkinhead, The Sawhorse, Woggle Bug, Tik Tok, Woozy, and Teddy Bear, but these characters did not appear in the film version of his book. Answer: L. Frank Baum (1856-1919)

5. This dad almost became a French writer instead of an English one. He was born in Russian Poland and spent most of his youth at sea. He had two sons. Answer: Joseph Conrad (1857-1924)

6. This pop earned a medical degree and based two of his most famous characters on his professors. He had two sons and one daughter. Answer: Sir Arthur Conan Doyle (1859-1930)

7. This dad worked as a night supervisor at a power plant. While at work he would turn a wheelbarrow upside down and write. He married a widow with two children. They had one child together. Answer: William Faulkner (1897-1962)

8. This father attended Princeton for four years but did not graduate. He applied for work at seven different newspapers—and all refused to hire him. Answer: F. Scott Fitzgerald (1896-1940)

9. This famous author unloaded bananas in New Orleans and was a bank teller in Austin, Texas. He served three years in the Ohio State Penitentiary. Answer: O. Henry (1862-1910)

10. This dad was a seaman, a cook, and a busboy. He was born in Missouri, and his mother was a schoolteacher. Answer: Langston Hughes (1902-1967)

11. This dad attended the Massachusetts Institute of Technology. While serving in World War I he wrote letters to his children, which included stories about the animals being used in the war, and he drew pictures to accompany the stories. Answer: Hugh Lofting (1886-1947). His letters were later turned into the Doctor Dolittle books.

12. This pop was the first American to win the Noble Prize for literature. He named his son Wells in honor of H. G. Wells. He attended Yale University but quit school and became a janitor. He tried to get a job helping to build the Panama Canal. He refused to accept the Pulitzer Prize. Answer: Sinclair Lewis (1885-1951)

13. This dad was born in Germany. He taught school and was a stonecutter in a cemetery. He also played the organ in a German mental hospital. The Germans burned his books in the 1930s. He lost his citizenship in Germany in 1938 and came to the United States in 1939. Answer: Erich Remarque (1897-1970)

14. This famous pop left school at age 13. His family name had been Johnson, but his father changed it. He worked as a bricklayer, a dishwasher, and a housepainter. He also fought in the Spanish American War. Answer: Carl Sandburg (1878-1967)

15. This dad wanted to attend the University of Michigan and play football. He also wanted to take dentistry courses. He became a reporter for a newspaper and covered the White Sox games. He became the editor of *Sporting News*. Answer: Ring Lardner (1885-1933)

THOSE WHO CAN... TEACH

THE IDEA
To promote the idea that teachers are capable, intelligent, talented people who can do other things, but choose to teach. This list of writers, all of whom began careers as teachers, may encourage students to enter the teaching or writing professions, or at least to develop a new admiration for their own teachers or one of the listed authors.

THE MATERIALS: Cover the bulletin board with bright paper or fabric. Add the caption "Those who can.... teach" and include pictures of some of the authors. You can use names from the list below or create your own list:

- Samuel Beckett
- Saul Bellow
- Gwendolyn Brooks
- Lewis Carroll
- Willa Cather
- Pat Conroy
- James Dickey
- Ralph Ellison
- Robert Frost
- William Golding
- Donald Hall
- James Hilton
- A. E. Housman
- James Weldon Johnson
- Sidney Lanier
- D. H. Lawrence
- Henry Wadsworth Longfellow
- Archibald MacLeish
- Bernard Malamud
- Marianne Moore
- Vladimir Nabokov
- Joyce Carol Oates
- Walter Pater
- Richard Peck
- Reynolds Price
- Theodore Roethke
- Louis Sachar
- J. R. R. Tolkein
- Alice Walker
- Robert Penn Warren
- Thornton Wilder
- Thomas Wolfe
- James Wright

WHAT'S IN A NAME?

THE IDEA To have students match the authors' pseudonyms with their birth names. Many authors have used their actual name *and* a pseudonym (or more than one). Students and faculty members may be surprised to discover that they have read a book and not realized that the pseudonym belonged to a writer with whom they were familiar. Students can use their research skills to match authors with their pen names.

 THE MATERIALS: Cover the bulletin board with colorful fabric or paper. Add the caption "What's in a name?" Use the list of authors' names below or create your own list. The words "pseudonym," "nom de plume," "pen name," and "alias" can be added to the board as vocabulary builders.

ACTUAL NAME	PSEUDONYM
Stephen King	Richard Bachman
Dean Koontz	David Axton
Agatha Christie	Mary Westmacott
Ray Bradbury	Douglas Spaulding
Korzeniowski	Joseph Conrad
Edna St. Vincent Millay	Nancy Boyd
William Sydney Porter	O. Henry
Theodore Geisel	Dr. Seuss
Eric Arthur Blair	George Orwell
L. Frank Baum	Edith Van Dyne
Charles Dickens	Boz Amandine
Aurore Lucile Dupin Dudevant	George Sand
Chloe Anthony Wofford	Toni Morrison
Howard Allen O'Brien	Anne Rice
Daniel Foe	Daniel Defoe

WHICH WAY DID THEY GO?

THE IDEA
To inform students and staff about the demise of well-known authors and writers.

THE MATERIALS: Cover the bulletin board with black paper. Add paper tombstones and list an author's name, and how he met his end, on each one. You may use names from the list below or create your own list:

■ *Ambrose Bierce:* Bierce probably died on the battlefield in Mexico. The exact conditions of his death are not known.

■ *Lord Byron:* He became ill and developed a fever after horseback riding in the rain. Doctors treated him with leeches, and he died soon afterward.

■ *Hart Crane:* Crane jumped overboard off the coast of Florida. He was presumed drowned.

■ *William Faulkner:* He was thrown from a horse and injured his back. Due to the back pain, he began drinking heavily. Shortly after, he suffered a fatal heart attack.

■ *Edgar Allan Poe:* For many years it was thought that Poe died from alcoholism, but authorities now think that he died from rabies.

■ *Percy Shelley:* Shelley drowned while sailing in Italy.

■ *Dylan Thomas:* Thomas died of pneumonia and from liver damage.

■ *Leo Tolstoy:* Tolstoy rode on an unheated train while attempting to leave Russia. He developed pneumonia and died.

■ *Oscar Wilde:* He developed an ear infection. When doctors operated, the infection spread into his brain.

WHAT DID THEY WANT TO BE?

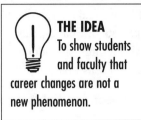

THE IDEA
To show students and faculty that career changes are not a new phenomenon.

THE MATERIALS: Cover the bulletin board with a colorful background. Add the caption "What did they want to be?" Add large pens, pencils, or cutouts of computer keyboards. Find writers who began careers in a different field, but wound up as successful and award-winning authors. The students can use their research skills to discover a writer's previous career. You can mix up the items in the list and have students match author with career, or you can simply post the list. You can use the list below or develop your own list.

Sherwood Anderson	Newspaper publisher
James Baldwin	Minister
Saul Bellow	Teacher
Robert Benchley	Actor
Anne Bronte	Governess
Charlotte Bronte	Governess
Gwendolyn Brooks	Teacher
Lewis Carroll	Teacher
Willa Cather	Teacher
Geoffrey Chaucer	Diplomat
Stephen Crane	Journalist
James Dickey	Teacher
Samuel Beckett	Teacher
Arthur Conan Doyle	Physician
Robert Frost	Teacher
Mark Twain	Journalist
Ernest Hemingway	Journalist
Jack London	Miner
William Shakespeare	Actor

WILL POWER!

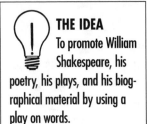

THE IDEA
To promote William Shakespeare, his poetry, his plays, and his biographical material by using a play on words.

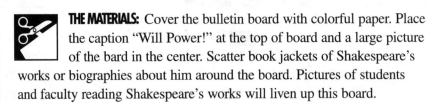

THE MATERIALS: Cover the bulletin board with colorful paper. Place the caption "Will Power!" at the top of board and a large picture of the bard in the center. Scatter book jackets of Shakespeare's works or biographies about him around the board. Pictures of students and faculty reading Shakespeare's works will liven up this board.

Idea suggested by Dianne Federovitch, Lovejoy (Georgia) High School

YOU DON'T KNOW JACK, IF YOU DON'T KNOW THESE

THE IDEA
To promote books written by people named "Jack," "Jackson," or something similar.

THE MATERIALS: Cover the board with a colorful fabric or paper. Cut your letters for the caption out in a coordinating color. The top caption "You don't know Jack" should be prominently displayed. The caption "if you don't know these" could be at the bottom of the board. Display book jackets written by authors whose name are Jack.

Sample list:
- Jack London
- Jack Higgins
- Jack Anderson
- Jack Conroy
- Jack Revell
- Jack Prelutsky

Dewey
Rules

A BLAST FROM THE PAST

THE IDEA
To encourage students to read both historical fiction and nonfiction dealing with our country's history.

THE MATERIALS: Cover the bulletin board with colorful fabric or paper. Add the caption "A Blast from the Past." Feature historical fiction titles and books dealing with the founding fathers, explorers, Pilgrims, and the westward expansion. Scatter "years" around the board to create more interest.

AS YOU SEW, SO SHALL YOU READ

THE IDEA
Use this caption to promote the sewing and craft books in your library media center.

THE MATERIALS: Cover the bulletin board with fabric or other material. Create the caption "As You Sew, So Shall You Read" with yarn glued to pieces of poster board or construction paper. The border is a continuation of the yarn. Place pictures of home economics students reading while sitting at sewing machines to add personality to the board. Add book jackets dealing with sewing and crafts to show students the wide variety of materials in your library media center.

BACK TO THE DRAWING BOARD

THE IDEA
To promote books on architecture, design, drawing, painting, or art.

THE MATERIALS: Cover the bulletin board with blue fabric or paper, or if available, use actual blueprints as the background (you may be able to find an architect who will donate some). Add the caption "Back to the Drawing Board" and book jackets about architecture, structural design, or art and artists.

BEEN THERE, READ THAT!

THE IDEA
To promote travel or geographical books. A vicarious vacation to places most of us will never travel can increase the circulation of the books about places, countries, and locales.

THE MATERIALS: Cover the bulletin board with a map of the world. If no map is available, cover the board with blue paper, then cut continent-shaped pieces of construction paper and place them on the background. Use the caption "Been There, Read That" to promote the books in your travel section. A smaller caption at the bottom of the board should read "And you don't need a ticket or a passport to travel." Add book jackets that feature exotic countries and foreign locales.

See appendix for an example of this bulletin board. (Chart D)

BOOK A TRIP

THE IDEA
To spotlight travel, geographical, and even astronomy books.

THE MATERIALS: Cover the bulletin board with blue paper or fabric. Add the caption "Book a Trip." Take digital pictures of students or ask them for school pictures. Create "passports" to place around the board and put the student photos in them. Add book jackets about countries, states, continents and even other planets.

CHECKOUT THESE TALL TALES

THE IDEA
To spotlight the 398 section of the library media center with the help of your school's basketball players. This is an overlooked section of most high school library media centers, but with a little "advertisement" its circulation should increase.

THE MATERIALS: Cover the board with colorful fabric or material. Take pictures of members of your school's basketball teams (both male and female) holding copies of tall-tale books. Add the caption "Checkout These Tall Tales" and place the pictures around the board.

CLOTHES CALLS!

THE IDEA
To promote the materials in your costume/fashion section (300s). This section of the library media center is used for periodic research, but most often is neglected. This board should get students' attention.

THE MATERIALS: Cover the bulletin board with colorful fabric. Add the caption "Clothes Calls!" and place book jackets about fashion, costumes, sewing, and manners of dress and attire around the board.

MEET SOMEONE NEW—READ A BIOGRAPHY

THE IDEA
To promote the biography section by spotlighting titles.

THE MATERIALS: Cover the bulletin board with brown paper or fabric (burlap makes an great backdrop to this board). Add a large scarecrow with a bushel basket full of leaves and book jackets of titles from the 920 or Biography section.

Idea suggested by Nancy Garabed, Terry Hallman & Marilyn Czekaj, Council Rock High School, Newtown, Pennsylvania

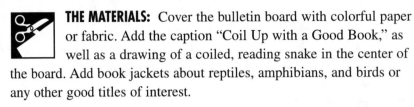
COIL UP WITH A GOOD BOOK

THE IDEA
To promote the books in the 500 section of your library media center.

THE MATERIALS: Cover the bulletin board with colorful paper or fabric. Add the caption "Coil Up with a Good Book," as well as a drawing of a coiled, reading snake in the center of the board. Add book jackets about reptiles, amphibians, and birds or any other good titles of interest.

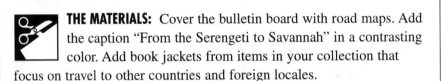
FROM THE SERENGETI TO SAVANNAH

THE IDEA
To promote travel books.

THE MATERIALS: Cover the bulletin board with road maps. Add the caption "From the Serengeti to Savannah" in a contrasting color. Add book jackets from items in your collection that focus on travel to other countries and foreign locales.

GET A LIFE

THE IDEA
To promote the reading of biographies.

THE MATERIALS: Cover the bulletin board with colorful fabric or paper. Add the caption "Get a Life." Attach biographical book jackets and photos of the people featured on the jackets.

Idea suggested by Julia Steger, Clifton Middle School, Covington, Virginia

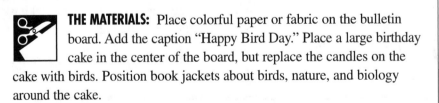
HAPPY BIRD DAY

THE IDEA
To promote books about birds, nature, and biology.

THE MATERIALS: Place colorful paper or fabric on the bulletin board. Add the caption "Happy Bird Day." Place a large birthday cake in the center of the board, but replace the candles on the cake with birds. Position book jackets about birds, nature, and biology around the cake.

HAVE A PETTY PROBLEM? SOLVE IT IN THE 600S!

THE IDEA
To promote the 600 section of the Dewey Decimal System.

THE MATERIALS: Cover the bulletin board with colorful paper or fabric. For a different look, you may want to use wrapping paper or fabric that has animals on it. Add the caption "Have a Petty Problem? Solve It in the 600s!" Attach book jackets that feature birds, cats, dogs, and gerbils, as well as pet care and veterinary science.

HIT ME WITH THE DEWEY DIGITS

THE IDEA
To spotlight certain nonfiction titles in your collection by emphasizing specific Dewey numbers.

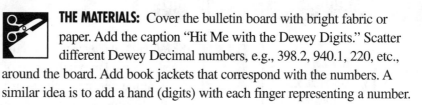

THE MATERIALS: Cover the bulletin board with bright fabric or paper. Add the caption "Hit Me with the Dewey Digits." Scatter different Dewey Decimal numbers, e.g., 398.2, 940.1, 220, etc., around the board. Add book jackets that correspond with the numbers. A similar idea is to add a hand (digits) with each finger representing a number.

SHORT, BUT SWEET

THE IDEA
To promote short stories, story collections, collected biographies, novellas, and poetry.

THE MATERIALS: Cover the board with colorful paper. Add the caption "Short, but Sweet" and jackets of books from your collection that meet the criteria for this theme. Attach "paper peppermints" to emphasize the "sweet"; the book jackets will let the students know the rest.

THE PAWS THAT REFRESHES

THE IDEA
To spotlight books about pets (dogs, cats, gerbils, hamsters) and books in the 600 section. This board could be incorporated with the "Match the Teachers to Their Pets" board.

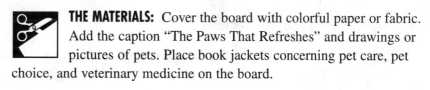

THE MATERIALS: Cover the board with colorful paper or fabric. Add the caption "The Paws That Refreshes" and drawings or pictures of pets. Place book jackets concerning pet care, pet choice, and veterinary medicine on the board.

THE STARS OF SCIENCE

THE IDEA
To promote biographies and other books about famous scientists from the 500 section.

THE MATERIALS: Cover the board with black fabric or paper. Add the caption "The Stars of Science" in metallic, yellow, or white paper, as well as paper or fabric stars. Place the name or a picture of a scientist inside each star. You may want to concentrate on a certain field of science, such as astronomy, or include scientists from all disciplines.

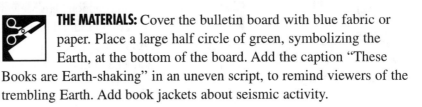

THESE BOOKS ARE EARTH-SHAKING

THE IDEA
To promote books from the 500 section on earthquakes, volcanoes, and other seismic activity.

THE MATERIALS: Cover the bulletin board with blue fabric or paper. Place a large half circle of green, symbolizing the Earth, at the bottom of the board. Add the caption "These Books are Earth-shaking" in an uneven script, to remind viewers of the trembling Earth. Add book jackets about seismic activity.

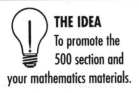

TOUCHED BY AN ANGLE

THE IDEA
To promote the 500 section and your mathematics materials.

THE MATERIALS: Cover the bulletin board with colorful fabric or paper. Add the caption "Touched by an Angle." Draw or use actual protractors, compasses, and rulers to add dimension to your board. Spotlight books from the mathematics section of your library media center.

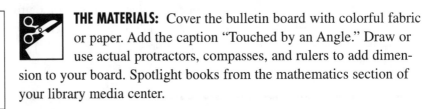

WE WANT YOUR BUSINESS

THE IDEA
To let students and staff know that they are welcome and wanted in the library media center.

THE MATERIALS: Cover the board with colorful fabric or paper. Add the caption "We Want Your Business" in large, bright letters. Add books and/or jackets of books dealing with careers in business and industry. Pictures of students and staff members using the library media center are ideal additions to this board, as are jackets from books in your collection.

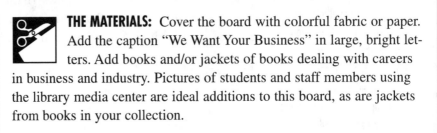

WELCOME BACH TO SCHOOL

THE IDEA
To promote the musical collection (700s) of your media center and have fun with a play on words.

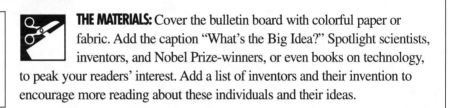

THE MATERIALS: Cover the board with colorful fabric or paper. Add the caption "Welcome Bach to School," along with a picture or portrait of Johann Sebastian Bach. Surround the board with jackets of titles from the music section of your collection. (You may want to add large musical notes to let students and staff know that you did not misspell any of the words in your caption.)

WHAT'S THE BIG IDEA?

THE IDEA
To promote books about inventors, inventions, and new ideas.

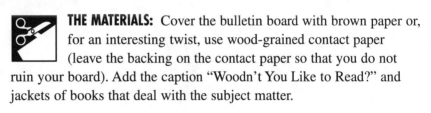

THE MATERIALS: Cover the bulletin board with colorful paper or fabric. Add the caption "What's the Big Idea?" Spotlight scientists, inventors, and Nobel Prize-winners, or even books on technology, to peak your readers' interest. Add a list of inventors and their invention to encourage more reading about these individuals and their ideas.

WOODN'T YOU LIKE TO READ?

THE IDEA
To promote reading about anything to do with wood: printing, forestry, refinishing, furniture making, bookmaking, and arts and craft.

THE MATERIALS: Cover the bulletin board with brown paper or, for an interesting twist, use wood-grained contact paper (leave the backing on the contact paper so that you do not ruin your board). Add the caption "Woodn't You Like to Read?" and jackets of books that deal with the subject matter.

Research
Rules

CHAPTER

8

THE BIG6™

The Big6 is an approach to teaching information and technology skills. It is used in many schools and in grades from kindergarten through college. The Big6 information problem-solving process is applicable wherever people need and use information. The Big6's creators, Mike Eisenberg and Bob Berkowitz, have granted us permission to use the following Big6-related bulletin board ideas in this book.

The Big6 skills are:

1 Task Definition
   a. Define the information problem
   b. Identify information needed in order to complete the task

2 Information Seeking Strategies
   a. Determine the range of possible sources (brainstorm)
   b. Evaluate the different possible sources to determine priorities (select the best sources)

3 Location and Access
   a. Locate sources (intellectually and physically)
   b. Find information within sources

4 Use of Information
   a. Engage (e.g., read, hear, view, touch) the information in a source
   b. Extract relevant information from a source

5 Synthesis
   a. Organize information from multiple sources
   b. Present the information

6 Evaluation
   a. Judge the product (effectiveness)
   b. Judge the information problem-solving process (efficiency)

IT'S ALWAYS TIME FOR THE BIG6

THE IDEA
To encourage students to use the Big6 ideas to write their essays, term papers, compositions, and themes, and to think about other ways the Big6 can help them in decision making.

THE MATERIALS: Cover the bulletin board with colorful paper or fabric. On the board have one step from the Big6 written on the face of each of six clocks. Point each clock's hands to the particular step number. For example, clock #1's hands would point to 1:00 and it would read, "Task Definition"; clock #2's hands would point to 2:00 and it would read, "Information Seeking Strategies"; clock #3's hands would point to 3:00 and it would read, "Location and Access"; and so on. Around the board scatter objects signifying events for which students can use the Big6 process, for example, choosing a college, buying a car, writing a research paper, or buying a gift for someone.

Idea suggested by Ann Gray, Pittsburg (New Hampshire) School

BIG6 SHOWERS

THE IDEA
To promote the Big6 Study Skills.

THE MATERIALS: The materials: Cover the bulletin board with blue fabric or paper. Add some fluffy white clouds and a large umbrella. On the handle of the umbrella write "The Big6." On cloud #1 write "The Big6…"; on cloud #2, "…showers you with…; on cloud #3, "good solutions to all of your information problems." Scatter raindrops over the rest of the board and label six of the drops with one each of the Big6 steps:

1 Task Definition
2 Information Seeking Strategies
3 Location and Access
4 Use of Information
5 Synthesis
6 Evaluation

Idea suggested by Ann Gray, Pittsburg (New Hampshire) School

COUNT ON THE BIG6

THE IDEA
To use the Big6 research skills in a Halloween theme.

THE MATERIALS: Cover the bulletin board with orange paper. Place a drawing of Count Dracula in the center. The caption on the board should read "Count on the Big6 to Help with Information Problems." Surround the Count with six numbered bats. Each bat has a banner flying behind it bearing one of the Big6 steps and a brief description of the step. Bat #1 would have Task Definition; bat #2, Information Seeking Strategies; bat #3, Location and Access; bat #4, Use of Information; bat #5, Synthesis; and bat #6, Evaluation.

Idea suggested by Ann Gray, Pittsburg (New Hampshire) School

DON'T MISS THE BUS—USE THE BIG6

THE IDEA
To encourage students to use the Big6 skills to have a successful school year.

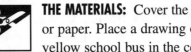

THE MATERIALS: Cover the bulletin board with colorful fabric or paper. Place a drawing or picture of the back of a large yellow school bus in the center of the board. Add drawings or actual pictures of students peering from the back of the bus. Attach six spiral notebooks around the board or use construction paper drawn to look like steno pads. Construct six paper pencils and place each one over a notebook (or pad). Write one of the Big6 steps on each pencil. The notebooks bear questions such as "What do I need to do?" for Task Definition, "What's the best place to find the information?" for Information Seeking Strategies, "Where can I find it?" for Location and Access, "How can I use it?" for Use of Information, "How can I put it together?" for Synthesis, and "How well did I do?" for Evaluation.

Idea suggested by Ann Gray, Pittsburg (New Hampshire) School

INFORMATION PROBLEMS?

THE IDEA
To help students use the Big6 to help find answers to their research questions.

THE MATERIALS: Cover the bulletin board with blue fabric or paper. Place pictures or silhouettes of two people (from the neck up), in winter gear, at opposite ends of the board. Add dialogue "bubbles" over each figure's head. The bubble over the person on the left reads, "Information problems got you snowed under?" The other person responds with, "Use the Big6 to shovel your way out." Add six snow shovels to the body of the board; label each one with one of the Big6 steps. Scatter paper snowflakes around the board.

Big6 steps:
1. Task Definition
2. Information Seeking Strategies
3. Location and Access
4. Use of Information
5. Synthesis
6. Evaluation

Idea suggested by Ann Gray, Pittsburg (New Hampshire) School

MAY THE SOURCE BE WITH YOU

THE IDEA
To promote your reference materials by using a play on words.

THE MATERIALS: Cover the bulletin board with a dark fabric or paper. Add the caption "May the Source Be with You." Complete the board by adding *Star Wars*-like characters or outer-space objects, such as stars, planets, satellites, or missiles, as well as jackets from, or pictures of, encyclopedias, dictionaries, atlases, or other reference materials.

SCOOP UP A WINNING YEAR

THE IDEA
To promote successful research strategies using the Big6 Skills.

THE MATERIALS: Cover the bulletin board with colorful fabric or paper. Use pictures or cutouts of four teenagers and a lot of paper ice cream cones for the focal point. Add speech "bubbles" for each character. One character says, "To meet success in the coming school year…" The next one says, "Scoop up some successful Information Seeking Strategies." The next one says, "Brainstorm a list of possible sources." And the last one says, "Then evaluate these sources to see which ones are the best." Surround the characters with variously flavored ice cream cones, labeled "encyclopedias," "books," "interviews," "field trips," "computers," "videos," and "periodicals."

Idea suggested by Ann Gray, Pittsburg (New Hampshire) School

THE WRITE WAY

THE IDEA
To promote materials that will help students compose more effective theses, themes, and research papers.

THE MATERIALS: Cover the bulletin board with black or green paper to resemble a chalkboard. Use chalk to hand-write the caption "The Write Way" in the center of the board. Surround the caption with jackets from books that discuss different types of writing formats, styles, and skills and strategies. Include examples of MLA and APA formats. (Hint: Spray the chalk with hair spray to prevent smearing.)

USE THE BIG6 TO LET IT R.I.P.

THE IDEA
To inspire students to use the Big6 problem-solving approach while sharing a little Halloween humor.

THE MATERIALS: Cover the bulletin board with black paper and place a Frankenstein-like figure in the center. Place tombstones around the monster. On the tombstones write messages such as, "Got one monster of an information problem? Use the Big6™ to let it R.I.P." Name the Big6 steps on paper bats, spiders, and cats, and scatter them around the graveyard. Add a large yellow moon for the final touch.

The Big6 skills are:

1 Task Definition
2 Information Seeking Strategies
3 Location and Access
4 Use of Information
5 Synthesis
6 Evaluation

Idea suggested by Gretchen Baldauf, Clinton Elementary School, West Seneca, New York

WHAT DO I DO NOW?

THE IDEA
Using the Big6 steps will help students decide to which colleges they should apply.

THE MATERIALS: Cover the bulletin board with colorful fabric or paper. Add the caption "What Do I Do Now?" Add silhouettes of a female and a male student wearing mortarboards. Scatter six "diplomas" on the board and label each with one of the Big6 steps:

Step 1: *Task Definition:* I need to choose a college.

Step 2: *Information Seeking Strategies:* Friends, guidance counselors, Internet, catalogs.

Step 3: *Location and Access:* Call friends, make an appointment with the counselors, go the library media center to access the Web and look through catalogs.

Step 4: *Use of Information:* Talk to the counselors, print information from the Web, use the college guides and take notes.

Step 5: *Synthesis:* Write to colleges, fill out financial aid forms, etc.

Step 6: *Evaluation:* Did I find all of the relevant information I needed? Am I happy with my choices?

Idea suggested by Ann Gray, Pittsburg (New Hampshire) School

Technology

CHAPTER 9

CHANGE YOUR PASSWORD AS OFTEN AS YOU CHANGE YOUR SOCKS

THE IDEA
To let students and faculty know how important it is to change their computer password frequently.

THE MATERIALS: Cover the bulletin board with colorful fabric or paper. Use actual socks to add dimension to the board. Write the caption, "Change Your Password as Often as You Change Your Socks," in a coordinating color to enhance visual impact.

DIGITAL BOY

THE IDEA
To use a song to inspire students to read and to use the library media center.

THE MATERIALS: Cover the bulletin board with black fabric or paper. Add the caption "21st-Century Digital Boy" (the title of song by a punk-rock band) and create the border using old CD-ROMs. Display technology books or book jackets from your collection.

Idea suggested by Sadie Longood, Dallas (Oregon) High School

FALL INTO THE NET

THE IDEA To combine an autumn theme with Web sites that will be helpful to your students. Use reliable search engines to surf the Net and you will find sites that can assist students with bibliographies, research, college planning, and much more. (Because the existence of sites can rapidly change, no actual URLs are included here.)

THE MATERIALS: Cover the board with orange, brown, or red paper or fabric, and add colorful fall leaves to make the border. Write the caption "Fall into the Net" and post useful URLs on the board.

FRIGHTENING FUTURE?

THE IDEA To promote fiction books that deal with technology, society, and the future.

THE MATERIALS: Cover the bulletin board with foil or metallic fabric. Add the caption "Frightening Future" or "Examine These Technology-Savvy Books." Add book jackets from books in your own collection or titles from the list below to create interest in books that deal with technology.

Suggested titles:

- *Armageddon Summer*/Coville & Yolen
- *Ender's Game*/Card
- *Ender's Shadow*/Card
- *Eva*/Dickinson
- *Gathering Blue*/Lowry
- *Idoru*/Gibson
- *I, Robot*/Asimov
- *The Martian Chronicles*/Bradbury
- *Stuck in Neutral*/Trueman
- *Terminal Experiment*/Sawyer
- *The Veldt*/Bradbury
- *Virtual War*/Skurzynski

GO SITE-SEEING

THE IDEA To promote quality, educational Web sites for students and staff.

THE MATERIALS: Cover the bulletin board with colorful paper. Make a "road" from black paper and place it on the board. Create small buildings from construction paper and place them along the "road." On each building write the address of a Web site that will interest teenagers. (Sites change frequently, so be sure to check each address to confirm that it is still accurate, before you post it on the board.) You could include the ALA site for teenagers, your school's site, or the sites of local industries and public libraries. Include college-related and career-related sites, as well as sites that offer studying tips.

THE HUNT IS ON

THE IDEA
To encourage students, especially seniors, to use Web sites to research colleges and universities, financial aid, scholarships, grants, and career choices.

THE MATERIALS: Cover the bulletin board with white paper and add cutouts of mortarboards as the border. Write the caption "The Hunt Is On" on the board. List the names and addresses of sites that can provide appropriate information to seniors who are trying to choose a college or are searching for scholarships. Use a list of sites that you have found or choose from the list below. (As always, make sure sites are appropriate for your needs and are still functioning.)

- CollegeNet <www.collegenet.com/>
- Campus Tours <www.campustours.com>
- FastWEB Scholarships Database <www.fastWeb.com/>
- Financial Aid Information Page <www.finaid.org>
- Kaplan's College Selector <www.csearch.kaplan.com>
- Peterson's <www.petersons.com>
- Recruiter USA <www.recruiterusa.com>

THE INFORMATION SUPERHIGHWAY

THE IDEA
To give the information superhighway a humorous and "human" touch by making your teachers part of this virtual thoroughfare.

THE MATERIALS: Cover the bulletin board with colorful paper. Add the caption "Look Who Is Cruising the Information Superhighway." Place a curving, black-construction-paper "road" across the board. Add variously sized clip-art printouts of vehicles, such as motorcycles, cars, and taxis. Collect small school photos of teachers, then cut out the teacher's face and put it in the windows (driver and passenger) of the vehicles. (Or use a digital camera to provide the same effect.) Place cutouts of stores and other buildings along the route and write the pertinent site addresses on the buildings.

Idea suggested by Sandi Dennis, Sims Elementary, Conyers, Georgia

TECHNOLOGY PUTS THE WORLD AT YOUR FINGERTIPS

 THE IDEA To promote the media center and fast-paced technological advances.

 THE MATERIALS: Cover the bulletin board with black fabric or paper. Use a silver border and, in white letters, add the caption "Technology Puts the World at Your Fingertips." Instead of using the word "world," create a "world" using poster board. Cut pictures of computers, cameras, scanners, printers, etc. out of technology magazines and add them to the board. Visit the computer lab and science labs, and take pictures of students using computers, camcorders, and digital cameras, then post those pictures, too. Place the caption "Our students are techno-savvy" at the bottom of the board and add old CD-ROMs for pizzazz.

Idea suggested by Christi Garner Unker, Carroll County High School, Carrollton, Kentucky

THESE KEYS WILL TAKE YOU PLACES

 THE IDEA To promote the computer keyboard, instead of the car keys, as a means of learning and exploration.

 THE MATERIALS: Cover the bulletin board with a bright fabric or color. Place a large drawing or poster of a computer keyboard in the center. Add the caption "These Keys Will Take You Places." Place pictures or book jackets of travel, biography, history, and animal books around the keyboard. Add a computer screen and mouse, if you wish.

THE WORLD'S FIRST SEARCH ENGINE: YOUR MEDIA CENTER

 THE IDEA To let students, staff, and faculty know that before there were search engines, people used the library media center to obtain information and to find research and reference materials, periodicals, and more.

 THE MATERIALS: Cover the bulletin board with colorful fabric or paper. Add the caption "The World's First Search Engine." In smaller letters, at the bottom of the board, write "Your Media Center." Add pictures of computers, books, and librarians/media specialists helping students find information. You can also feature tidbits of information about the history of the library.

Interactive

AND THAT'S FINAL!

THE IDEA Take the final words from works of classic literature and from students' favorite titles to create a bulletin board that challenges students and faculty to determine which book ends with which sentence.

THE MATERIALS: Choose books from your collection and write down their final sentences. Then, create two lists: one of the books' final words and one of the books' titles. (Or use the list below.) You can post both the "quotes" list and the "answers" list on the board, or you can post only the "quotes" list and have students use their research skills to find the answers.

FINAL SENTENCE	BOOK
"When we reach the city."	*Farenheit 451*/Bradbury
"Whatever we had missed, we possessed together the precious, the incommunicable past."	*My Antonia*/Cather
"But the provoking kitten only began on the other paw, and pretended it hadn't heard the question."	*Alice in Wonderland*/Carroll
"But he did not ask, and his uncle did not speak except to say, after a few minutes, 'It's time to go home,' and all the way home they walked in silence."	*A Death in the Family*/Agee
"O, my girls, however long you may live, I never can wish you a greater happiness than this!"	*Little Women*/Alcott
"Daily he announces more distinctly,—'Surely, I come quickly!' and hourly I more eagerly respond,—'Amen,' even so come, Lord Jesus."	*Jane Eyre*/Bronte
"It was an old chant, a very old one, and he sang it not to the evening but to himself, to be sure he had not forgotten the words, to be sure he would never again forget."	*When the LegendsDie*/Borland

THE IDEA
Many books are easily recognizable by their first sentence. Have students and faculty members attempt to identify titles by their famous first line.

THE MATERIALS: Cover the bulletin board with colorful material. Add the caption "It Was a Dark and Stormy Night." Create a list of memorable first lines and have students use their research skills to determine which book each line is from. You can provide a list of titles so students can match title and line, or simply list the first line. Use the list below or create your own list using students' favorite titles.

FIRST SENTANCE	BOOK
"The boy with fair hair lowered himself down the last few feet of rock and began to pick his way towards the lagoon."	*Lord of the Flies*/Golding
"To the red country and part of the gray country of Oklahoma, the last rains came gently, and they did not cut the scarred earth."	*The Grapes of Wrath*/Steinbeck
"Mother died today."	*The Stranger*/Golding
"It was Wang Lung's marriage day."	*The Good Earth*/Buck
"He sat in defiance of municipal orders, astride the gun of Zam-Zammeh on her brick platform opposite the old Ajaibher-the Wonder House, as the natives called the Lahore Museum."	*Kim*/Kipling
"It was the best of times, it was the worst of times, it was the age of wisdom, it was the age of foolishness, it was the epoch of belief, it was the epoch of incredulity, it was the season of Light, it was the season of Darkness, it was the spring of hope, it was the winter of despair, we had everything before us, we had nothing before us, we were all going direct to Heaven, we were all going direct the other way—in short, the period was so."	*A Tale of Two Cities*/Dickens
"It is a truth universally acknowledged, that a single man in possession of a good fortune, must be in want of a wife."	*Pride and Prejudice*/Austen
"My father's family name being Pirrip, and my Christian name Philip, my infant tongue could make of both names nothing longer or more explicit than Pip."	*Great Expectations*/Dickens
"Now, what I want is Facts."	*Hard Times*/Dickens
"There was no possibility of taking a walk that day."	*Jane Eyre*/Bronte

HERSTORY

THE IDEA
To celebrate Women's History Month create a bulletin board with questions about women's role in literature, politics, theater, science, and other fields. Choose questions that students can find answers to by using the library media center.

THE MATERIALS: Cover the bulletin board with colorful fabric or paper and add the caption "Herstory" (instead of "History"). Write each question on a separate piece of paper and attach the papers to the board. You may want to offer a prize to the student who can answer the most questions in a predetermined amount of time.

Sample questions:

1. Who was the first female United States attorney general? (Janet Reno)

2. Who was the first American woman in space? (Sally Ride)

3. The first bridge in the United States named for a woman joins Pennsauken, New Jersey, and Philadelphia. For whom it is named? (Betsy Ross)

4. This person was the first woman to serve as both a congresswoman and a senator. She also was the first woman to seek the presidency. What is her name? (Margaret Chase Smith [1897-1995])

5. Who was the first woman to run for Congress? (Elizabeth Cady Stanton [1815-1902])

6. What was Harriet Tubman's name at birth? (Araminta)

7. Alice Walker, author of *The Color Purple*, attended what colleges? (Spelman and Sarah Lawrence)

8. Ida Bell Wells-Barnett helped form the NAACP and the first black woman's suffrage association. What was the suffrage association called? (Alpha Suffrage Club)

9. Who was the first black woman to publish a book of poetry in the United States? (Phillis Wheatley)

10. Who were the country's first female governors? (Nellie Tayloe Ross, Wyoming, 1924; Miriam Amanda "Ma" Ferguson, Texas, 1924)

THE LOVE CONNECTION

THE IDEA
To encourage students and staff to use their research skills to match lovers from literature and real life.

THE MATERIALS: Cover the bulletin board with red fabric or paper. Add the caption "The Love Connection." Create your own list of famous lovers or use the list of sweethearts below. You may want to offer a prize to the student who can correctly match the names on the list.

1. Desdemona	A. Duke of Windsor
2. Calpurnia	B. Othello
3. Portia	C. Agamemnon
4. Juliet	D. Ashley Wilkes
5. Ophelia	E. Lancelot
6. Hester Prynne	F. Professor Higgins
7. Beatrice	G. Aeneas
8. Jocasta	H. Menelaus
9. Penelope	I. Jay Gatsby
10. Rosalind	J. Oedipus Rex
11. Elizabeth	K. Prince Albert
12. Zelda	L. Dante
13. Catherine	M. Hamlet
14. Daisy	N. Rhett Butler
15. Victoria	O. Don Quixote
16. Eliza Doolittle	P. King Priam
17. Nancy	Q. F. Scott Fitzgerald
18. Guinevere	R. Julius Caesar
19. Scarlett	S. Arthur Dimmesdale
20. Melanie	T. Romeo
21. Wallace Simpson	U. Heathcliff
22. Clytemnestra	V. Ronnie
23. Eurydice	W. Robert Browning
24. Ariadne	X. Odysseus
25. Helen of Troy	Y. Porgy
26. Hecuba	Z. Theseus
27. Dido	AA. Brutus
28. Dulcinea	BB. Orpheus
29. Mary	CC. Percy Bysshe Shelley
30. Bess	DD. Orlando

Answers:

1. Desdemona/Othello
2. Calpurnia/Julius Caesar
3. Portia/Brutus
4. Juliet/Romeo
5. Ophelia/Hamlet
6. Hester Prynne/Arthur Dimmesdale
7. Beatrice/Dante
8. Jocasta/Oedipus Rex
9. Penelope/Odysseus
10. Rosalind/Orlando
11. Elizabeth/Robert Browning
12. Zelda/F. Scott Fitzgerald
13. Catherine/Heathcliff
14. Daisy/Jay Gatsby
15. Victoria/Prince Albert
16. Eliza Doolittle/Professor Higgins
17. Nancy/Ronnie
18. Guinevere/Lancelot
19. Scarlett/Rhett Butler
20. Melanie/Ashley Wilkes
21. Wallace Simpson/Duke of Windsor
22. Clytemnestra/Agamemnon
23. Eurydice/Orpheus
24. Ariadne/Theseus
25. Helen of Troy/Menelaus
26. Hecuba/King Priam
27. Dido/Aeneas
28. Dulcinea/Don Quixote
29. Mary/Percy Bysshe Shelley
30. Bess/Porgy

Idea suggested by Dianne Federovitch, Lovejoy (Georgia) High School

TAKE THE DIVA CHALLENGE

THE IDEA
To promote Women's History Month and to encourage students to use the library media center to locate the answers to these questions.

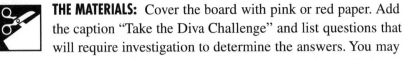

THE MATERIALS: Cover the board with pink or red paper. Add the caption "Take the Diva Challenge" and list questions that will require investigation to determine the answers. You may want to offer prizes to the students who can correctly answer the most questions. Make up your own questions, using research materials available to your students and staff, or use the questions listed below:

1. Who is Maya Lin?
2. Who is Susan Cobb Milton Atkinson?
3. Who is Madeline Albright?
4. What did Pancho (Florence) Lowe Barnes do that was interesting?
5. Who is Daisy Lee Gatson Bates?
6. Why is Clara Hale important?
7. Who was the first female professor at Harvard?
8. Who said "Remember the ladies" to her husband when he was helping to create the new nation of the United States?
9. Who was the first female member of a presidential cabinet?
10. Who was the first woman associate justice of the United States Supreme Court?
11. Who is Elsie De Wolfe?

Answers:

1. Maya Lin is the sculptor who designed the poignant Vietnam Veterans Memorial. At only 21 years of age, Lin received national attention as the artist who had been commissioned to create the Washington, D.C., memorial. Widely criticized at first, Lin's creation quickly became one of the most highly respected works of public art—and the most-visited public monument—in the United States.

2. Susan Cobb Milton Atkinson helped found Georgia Normal and Industrial School, which later became Georgia College.

3. Madeline Albright was the first female secretary of state.

4. Pancho (Florence) Lowe Barnes was the first woman stunt pilot.

5. Daisy Lee Gatson Bates was a civil rights activist.

6. Clara Hale is a child advocate. She founded Hale House and cared for hundreds of children.

7. Alice Hamilton was the first female professor at Harvard.

8. Abigail Adams

9. Frances Perkins was the first female member of a president's cabinet.

10. Sandra Day O'Connor was the first associate justice of the Supreme Court.

11. Elsie De Wolfe was an actress, a socialite, and the inventor of interior design.

TWENTY QUESTIONS

THE IDEA To promote Black History Month by posing questions dealing with important African-American people, literature, and facts. Students should be able to find all of the answers to the questions in the library media center. You may want to offer a prize to the student who can correctly answer the most questions in a designated time period.

THE MATERIALS: Cover the bulletin board with colorful fabric or paper. The caption could read "Twenty Questions."

Sample questions:

1 Martin Luther King was such a good dresser as a young man that his nickname was _____.

2 Who was the first African-American woman to have a nonfiction book on the best-seller list?

3 Who was the first African-American dramatist to win the Pulitzer Prize for drama?

4 Who was the first African American to win an Oscar?

5 What was ironic about Dr. Charles Drew's death?

6 Who was the first African American to sing a principal role at the Metropolitan Opera?

7 Who was the first African-American singer with the Grand Ole Opry?

8 Who was the first African-American man to host a nationally broadcast television talk show?

9 Who was the first African-American president of the Atlanta Board of Education?

10 Who founded *Ebony* and *Jet* magazines?

11 Who was the first African-American woman to win an Emmy award?

12 Who is Roland Hayes and where is he from?

13 Where was Phillis Wheatley born?

14 Who was the first African-American woman to win the Pulitzer Prize for fiction?

15 What was Martin Luther King's name when he was born?

16 Who was the first black to play Othello on an American stage with a white cast?

17 Who was the first African American to win the New York Drama Critics Award?

18 Which was the first colony to abolish slavery?

19 Who founded the Children's Defense Fund?

20 Who was the first African American to earn a Ph.D. from Harvard?

Answers on the following page

Answers:

1. "Tweed"

2. Maya Angelou

3. Charles Gardone

4. Hattie McDaniel

5. Charles Drew started the "Blood for Britain" project in 1940, which consisted of collecting and drying blood plasma to be used for transfusions on the battlefield. In April 1950 he was killed in an auto accident in North Carolina. The segregated hospital to which he was admitted did not have any blood plasma that might have saved his life.

6. Marian Anderson

7. Charlie Pride

8. Arsenio Hall

9. Benjamin Mays

10. John H. Johnson

11. Gail Fisher

12. Roland Hayes was the first African American to sing in Symphony Hall in Boston. He was born in Curryville, Georgia.

13. Phillis Wheatley was born on the west coast of Africa.

14. Alice Walker

15. Michael

16. Paul Robeson

17. Lorraine Hansberry

18. Vermont, in 1777

19. Marian Wright Edelman

20. W. E. B. DuBois

WHAT'S THE CONNECTION?

THE IDEA
To encourage students to use research skills to answer questions.

THE MATERIALS: Cover the bulletin board with colorful paper. Add the caption "What's the Connection?" Use the list of items below, all of which have a common link, or create your own list of items. Challenge students and staff to find the answers.

Escalator	High octane	Trampoline	Cube steak	Raisin bran
Cornflakes	Linoleum	Yo-yo	Dry ice	Kerosene
Lanolin	Mimeograph	Nylon	Shredded wheat	

The connection among the items listed above is that all were once trademarked names, but lost their trademark for various reasons. Other ideas for lists are "books that have been banned in your community," "authors who were former teachers," etc.

WHEN IN THE WORLD?

THE IDEA List common inventions or products and have students and faculty use their research skills to determine in which decade the products became generally accessible to the public.

THE MATERIALS: Cover the bulletin board with colorful material or paper. Add the caption "When in the World?" and scatter large question marks around the board. Place the product names and their "years" randomly and separately on the board. Use the list of products below or create your own list:

1870s	Blue jeans		Barbed wire		
1900s	BB guns				
1910s	Road maps	Margarine	Motorcycles	Jell-O	Ice cream cones
1920s	Aspirin	Yo-yos	Band-Aids	Bubble gum	Potato chips
1930s	Comic books	Monopoly	Popsicles	Zippers	
1940s	Frozen foods		Frozen orange juice		
1950s	Frisbees		Scrabble game		
1960s	Contact lenses	Photocopiers	Color TVs	Scuba diving equipment	
1970s	Antiperspirants	Pocket calculators		Velcro	

WHO INVENTS WORDS?

THE IDEA To inform students and faculty about words that have been introduced into our language by authors.

THE MATERIALS: This bulletin board could be both an informative board and an interactive one. List the authors, their titles, and their inventive word, and have students use their research skills to determine who introduced the word into our vocabulary. The caption, "Who Invents Words?" should be centered on the board, and the authors' names, titles, and words should be listed in a chart format. You can use the words from the list below or, using materials from your library media center, develop your own list.

AUTHOR	TITLE	NEW WORD
Jonathan Swift	*Gulliver's Travels*	yahoo
Lewis Carroll	*Through the Looking Glass*	chortle
John Milton	*Paradise Lost*	pandemonium
Miguel de Cervantes	*Don Quixote*	quixotic
Moliere	*La Princesse d'Elide*	moron
Shakespeare	*The Merchant of Venice*	shylock
Thomas More	*Utopia*	utopian
James Hilton	*Lost Horizon*	Shangri-La
James Joyce	*Finnegan's Wake*	quark

WHO READS WHAT?

THE IDEA
To let students and teachers know what celebrities might enjoy reading. Students might become interested enough in a personalitiy's favorite titles to read the books themselves.

THE MATERIALS: Cover the bulletin board with colorful paper or fabric. Choose some well-known people and find out their favorite book. Pictures or photographs of the celebrity will add interest to the board. Also include a book jacket or picture of the book. You could create a contest and have the students try to figure out what book goes with which person.

Sample list:

CELEBRITY	FAVORITE TITLE
Jimmy Carter	*Let Us Now Praise Famous Men*/Agee & Evans
Whoopi Goldberg	*To Kill a Mockingbird*/Lee
Charles Schultz	*The Silver Skates*/Dodge
Gloria Steinem	*The Color Purple*/Walker
Ann Landers	*The Scarlet Letter*/Hawthorne
Arsenio Hall	*Little Girl Lost*/Barrymore
Laila Ali	*The Color Purple*/Walker
Tim Allen	*Zen and the Art of Motorcycle Maintenance*/Pirsig
Alec Baldwin	*To Kill a Mockingbird*/Lee
Tyra Banks	*Are You There God? It's Me, Margaret*/Blume
Halle Berry	*Are You There God? It's Me, Margaret*/Blume
Norman Schwarzkopf	*White Fang*/London
Aaron Spelling	*The Catcher in the Rye*/Salinger
Steven Spielberg	*The Last of the Mohicans*/Cooper
The Rock	*I Have a Dream: The Life and Times of Martin Luther King*/Davis
Rosie O'Donnell	*The Catcher in the Rye*/Salinger
Stephen King	*Lord of the Flies*/Golding
Bette Midler	*Alice in Wonderland*/Carroll
Alex Haley	*The Old Man and the Sea*/Hemingway
Whitney Houston	*Yes, I Can: The Story of Sammy Davis, Jr.*/Davis
Gloria Estefan	*A Tree Grows in Brooklyn*/Smith
Drew Bledsoe	*Robinson Crusoe*/Defoe
Levar Burton	*Captains Courageous*/Kipling
Tom Clancy	*20,000 Leagues Under the Sea*/Verne

WHO SAID IT?

THE IDEA
To test students' knowledge of the correct origins of famous quotations that are commonly credited to other people.

THE MATERIALS: Cover the board with paper or material. Add the caption "Who Said It?" and put large question marks randomly around the board. Use the following list of quotations or create your own list. You may want to provide a list of possible answers or let students use their research skills to find the correct answers.

QUOTE	WHO SAID IT?
"Anybody who hates children and dogs can't be all bad."	Leo Rosten
"Go west, young man."	John Soule
"Everybody talks about the weather, but nobody does anything about it."	Charles Dudley Warner
"Survival of the fittest."	Herbert Spencer
"That government is best which governs least."	Henry David Thoreau

THE IDEA
Many authors use three names. This bulletin board encourages students to learn writers' full names—first, last, and middle.

THE MATERIALS: Cover the bulletin board with colorful paper or fabric. Add the caption "Who's in the Middle?" Post the authors' middle names and let students and staff determine each writer's first and last name. Use the list below or create one of your own.

_____	Allan	_____
_____	Anne	_____
_____	Beecher	_____
_____	Bernard	_____
_____	Booth	_____
_____	Butler	_____
_____	Carlos	_____
_____	Chandler	_____
_____	Clarke	_____
_____	Conan	_____
_____	Cullen	_____
_____	David	_____
_____	Laurence	_____
_____	Lee	_____
_____	Makepeace	_____
_____	May	_____
_____	Neale	_____
_____	Penn	_____
_____	Rice	_____
_____	St. Vincent	_____
_____	Wadsworth	_____
_____	Waldo	_____
_____	Whitcomb	_____

Answers on the following page

WHO'S IN THE MIDDLE? (cont.)

Answers:

Edgar Allan Poe
Katherine Anne Porter
Harriet Beecher Stowe
George Bernard Shaw
Clare Booth Luce
William Butler Yeats
William Carlos Williams
Joel Chandler Harris
Clement Clarke Moore
Arthur Conan Doyle
William Cullen Bryant
Henry David Thoreau

Paul Laurence Dunbar
Edgar Lee Masters
William Makepeace Thackery
Louisa May Alcott
Zora Neale Hurston
Robert Penn Warren
Edgar Rice Burroughs
Edna St. Vincent Millay
Henry Wadsworth Longfellow
Ralph Waldo Emerson
James Whitcomb Riley

MATCH THE TEACHER WITH HER PET

THE IDEA
To spotlight the animal lovers among the faculty. This would be a great board for National Library Week.

THE MATERIALS: Cover the bulletin board with a colorful fabric or paper. Ask teachers for a photograph of themselves and a photograph of their pet. Ask students and staff to match the owner with the animal. When teachers see the interest this board generates, they will want to submit their pictures, too.

Idea suggested by Sadie Longood, Dallas (Oregon) High School

Strictly Teens

DON'T READ THESE BOOKS

THE IDEA
To promote Banned Book Week

THE MATERIALS: Cover the bulletin board with black paper or fabric. In yellow, add the caption "Don't Read These Books." Use yellow caution tape for the border and add titles from your collection that have been banned in some communities (or use authors and titles from the list below). Authors whose work has been challenged or banned include:

Authors:

Maya Angelou
Piers Anthony
Judy Blume
Caroline Cooney
Robert Cormier
Lois Duncan
Lois Lowry
Walter Dean Myers
Phylis Reynolds Naylor
J. K. Rowling
John Steinbeck
Paul Zindel

Titles:

I Know Why the Caged Bird Sings/Angelou
Harry Potter/Rowling
The Chocolate War/Cormier
Killing Mr. Griffin/Duncan
Of Mice and Men/Steinbeck
Fallen Angels/Myers
The Giver/Lowry
To Kill a Mockingbird/Lee
Huckleberry Finn/Twain
Catcher in the Rye/Salinger

HAVE YOU READ THESE BOOKS?

THE IDEA To promote Banned Books Week and inform students and staff about how frequently materials are challenged.

THE MATERIALS: Cover the bulletin board with gray fabric or paper. Add jackets or titles of challenged or banned books. Place vertical bars in front of the titles to suggest a jail cell. Add the caption "Have You Read These Books?" In smaller letters, write, "Some People Don't Want You To." Use books from your collection or use titles from the list below:

Challenged books/authors:

- *The Adventures of Huckleberry Finn*/Twain
- *Blubber*/Blume
- *The Bluest Eye*/Morrison
- *Bridge to Terabithia*/Paterson
- *The Catcher in the Rye*/Salinger
- *A Day No Pigs Would Die*/Peck
- *Flowers for Algernon*/Keyes

- *Go Ask Alice*/Anonymous
- *Of Mice and Men*/Steinbeck
- *My Brother Sam Is Dead*/Collier
- *The Outsiders*/Hinton
- *The Pigman*/Zindel
- *To Kill a Mockingbird*/Lee
- *A Wrinkle in Time*/L'Engle

BE SEEN WITH PRINT

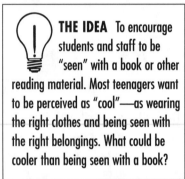

THE IDEA To encourage students and staff to be "seen" with a book or other reading material. Most teenagers want to be perceived as "cool"—as wearing the right clothes and being seen with the right belongings. What could be cooler than being seen with a book?

THE MATERIALS: Cover the board with a colorful fabric or paper. Add the caption "Be Seen with Print." Take pictures of a variety of students (different grade levels, male/female, different ethnicities, athletes, honor students, and everyone in between) reading a book, then place the photos on the board. As a special feature, quote some of the students explaining why they like being "seen with print."

BUMPER STICKERS FOR LIBRARY LOVERS

THE IDEA Bumper stickers are everywhere. But what if library media specialists designed bumper stickers? What would they say? You can use these ideas, use your own, or ask students to give you creative notions.

THE MATERIALS: Cover the bulletin board with colorful paper or fabric. Draw or cut out the general shape of a car bumper and place it at the top of the board. Cut another sheet of paper in the shape of a bumper sticker, write the caption "Bumper Stickers for Library Lovers" on it, and "stick" it to the bumper. Attach additional bumper-sticker slogans around the board.

Suggested slogans:

- If you can read this, check out a book.
- Don't blame me, I read.
- I carry a library card.
- I brake for books.

- I'd rather be reading.
- I'm an honor student because I read.
- So many books, so little time
- I think. Therefore, I read.

CAREERS

THE IDEA This student-inspired bulletin board began as an assignment to create a board to promote vocation/career week.

THE MATERIALS: A quote from Buddha, "Your work is to discover our work, and then with all your heart to give yourself to it," was placed in the center of the board. Actual shoes that typified different kinds of work were placed around the board's edges. The types of shoes used included firefighters' boots, nurses' shoes, ballet slippers, high heels, construction boots, wing tips, and others.

Idea suggested by Susan Ryan, Lovejoy (Georgia) High School

DO YOU KNOW A HERO?

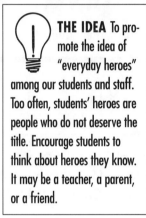

THE IDEA To promote the idea of "everyday heroes" among our students and staff. Too often, students' heroes are people who do not deserve the title. Encourage students to think about heroes they know. It may be a teacher, a parent, or a friend.

THE MATERIALS: Cover the board with colorful paper. Add the caption "Do You Know a Hero? Tell Them and Then Tell the World." Include a large question mark in the center of the board. Find information about real heroes and post that information on the bulletin board.

Sample list:
- Jim Abbott
- Marion Anderson
- Arthur Ashe
- Jim & Sarah Brady
- Jimmy & Rosalyn Carter
- Clara Hale
- Wilma Mankiller
- Chico Mendes
- J. Robert Oppenheimer
- Colin Powell
- Wilma Rudolph
- Albert Schweitzer
- Corrie Ten Boom
- Ryan White
- Flight 93 passengers
- The firefighters, police officers, and EMTs at the World Trade Center

FEELING DOWN?

THE IDEA To let students and staff know that everyone suffers failures and disappointments, but that these setbacks do not have to prevent you from succeeding.

THE MATERIALS: Cover the bulletin board with colorful paper. Add the caption "Feeling Down?" Using biographical sources, find and post information about successful people's "failures," or use examples from the list below:

Sample list:

- Robin Williams was voted "Least Likely to Succeed" in high school.
- Albert Einstein was a poor student.
- Orville Wright was expelled from the sixth grade for bad behavior.
- Michael Jordan did not make his high school team in the 10th grade. The coach thought that he was not good enough.
- Ted Turner was suspended twice from Brown University.
- Charles Schultz's cartoons were rejected by his high school yearbook.
- Mickey Mantle struck out 710 times.
- Whoopi Goldberg is a high school dropout.
- Emily Dickinson wrote about 1,800 poems. Only seven were published during her lifetime.

THE FUTURE IS CLEAR

THE IDEA To show students that library media center resources can help them see, clarify, and plan their future.

THE MATERIALS: Cover the bulletin board with cellophane, plastic wrap, or any see-through material. Using brightly colored paper add the caption "The Future Is Clear." Add book jackets about college and career choices.

GOTCHA!*

THE IDEA To promote and highlight students who do a good job, whether in the classroom, in the hallways, at lunch, or in a club.

THE MATERIALS: Cover the board with black fabric or paper. Add the caption "Gotcha!" in large letters and a card that explains what is required to get one's name on the Gotcha! board. The requirements can include actions such as helping someone in the hallway, picking up trash that does not belong to you, showing consideration and thoughtfulness to others, making progress in your academic subjects, etc. Teachers can let you know what students are to be included on the board. You may choose to take pictures of the students and post the photos on the board or to put the students' names on a card.

*Creating this board requires the cooperation of the faculty and staff.

IT'S A TEEN THING

THE IDEA
To spotlight teenagers in the media and periodicals.

THE MATERIALS: Cover the board with wild fabric or a bright color. Add the caption "It's a teen thing." Find interesting and informative articles about teenagers in the newspaper, magazines, or books. You may want to feature teenagers from your school who have been in the news. Spotlight teen-interest magazines to which your library media center subscribes and watch your magazine circulation increase!

MISSING SOMETHING?

THE IDEA
To show students that without their library media center, something important would be missing from their lives.

THE MATERIALS: Cover the bulletin board with dark paper. Draw the outline of a person on construction paper, then cut this shape into puzzle-shaped pieces. Even though the shape is a simple outline drawing, should be colorful. Put the figure together on the bulletin board, but place one or two of the puzzle pieces apart from the shape. Surround the "puzzle person" with book jackets. You could even create your person from book jackets glued to cardboard and then cut out in a human shape.

PLANET HIGH SCHOOL

THE IDEA
Students may think the world revolves around their high school; this bulletin board may confirm that belief.

THE MATERIALS: Cover the bulletin board with black fabric or paper. Add the caption "Planet High School," inserting the name of your school to personalize it. Cut out a large circular "planet" and place it in the center of the board. Color the "planet" in your school colors and add jackets of books about teenage issues.

READING RULES!

THE IDEA
To promote reading in a humorous manner. Students have to deal with rules and regulations all the time, but these rules should bring a smile to students' faces.

THE MATERIALS: Use colorful fabric or paper to cover the bulletin board and add the caption "John Cotton Dana's Reading Rules." Add these 12 rules:

1. Read
2. Read
3. Read some more
4. Read anything
5. Read about everything
6. Read enjoyable things
7. Read things you yourself enjoy
8. Read, and talk about it
9. Read very carefully, some things
10. Read on the run, most things
11. Don't think about reading, but
12. Just read

SENIORS AND SENIORS

THE IDEA
To promote the senior class and senior citizens by displaying photographs of members of the senior class with their grandparents

THE MATERIALS: Cover the bulletin board with colorful fabric or paper. Add the caption "Seniors and Seniors." This board requires advance planning. You will need to ask some students to bring pictures of themselves and their grandparents. You could use this board if your school has a special event for senior citizens, on Grandparents Day or just to salute special members of our society.

SO MANY BOOKS, SO LITTLE TIME

THE IDEA
To promote the library media center collection.

THE MATERIALS: Cover the bulletin board with colorful paper or fabric. Add the caption "So Many Books, So Little Time." Add a real or paper clock and the number of books in your collection. Most secondary students are only in high school for three to four years, so emphasize that time is of the essence if they want to read all of the titles your center offers.

SPRING BREAK

THE IDEA
Students are always excited about spring break, whether they head for the beach or vacation at home. This reminder about what to pack may encourage them to take along a book.

THE MATERIALS: Cover the bulletin board with blue paper for the sky, brown for a sandy beach, and green for the ocean. Place the caption "Spring Break" at the top of the board. In the center of the board add a colorful umbrella with a pair of legs poking out from underneath it. Place an additional caption at the bottom that reads, "Don't forget the beach, your bathing suit, and your book."

STRESSED FOR SUCCESS

THE IDEA
To promote career- and college-oriented reading material. The month of February is a stressful time for seniors. Deadlines for college applications, financial forms, and scholarships, as well as having to cope with the last semester before graduation, can all be causes of anxiety for teens.

THE MATERIALS: Place a large dollar sign ($) in the center of the bulletin board, surrounded by the caption "Stressed for Success." Add materials about careers, scholarships, SAT testing, and other items that seniors will find helpful as they make career and college decisions.

Idea submitted by Sadie Longood, Dallas (Oregon) High School

THREE WORDS TO HELP YOU SUCCEED IN HIGH SCHOOL

THE IDEA
Students must walk up to and touch this bulletin board if they want to know the three words.

THE MATERIALS: Cover the bulletin board with colorful fabric or paper. Add the caption "Three Words to Help You Succeed in High School" in large letters. Fold three sheets of construction paper in half and attach them to the board underneath the caption. Inside each folded piece of paper write the word, "Read." So, how do you become successful? Read, read, read.

TIRED OF TESTS? THEN TAKE THIS QUIZ!

THE IDEA
This "quiz" reminds students and staff of the really important things in life.

THE MATERIALS: Cover the bulletin board with colorful paper. Add the caption "Tired of Tests? Then Take This Quiz." Place these two "quizzes" on your bulletin board.

Quiz #1:

1 Name the five wealthiest people in the world.

2 Name the last five Heisman trophy winners.

3 Name the last five winners of the Miss America contest.

4 Name 10 people who have won the Nobel or Pulitzer Prize.

5 Name the last six Academy Award-winners for best actor and actress.

6 Name the World Series winners for the past 10 years.

How did you do?

The point is that none of us remember the headliners of yesterday. These are not second-rate achievers—they are the best in their fields. But the applause dies. Awards tarnish. Achievements are forgotten. Accolades and certificates are buried with their owners.

Quiz #2:

1 List a few teachers who aided your journey through school.

2 Name three friends who have helped you through a difficult time.

3 Name five people who have taught you something worthwhile.

4 Think of people who have made you feel appreciated and special.

5 Think of five people who enjoy spending time with.

Easier?

The lesson: The people who make a difference in your life are not the ones with the most credentials, the most money, or the most awards. They are the ones who care.

Idea from *The City of Jonesboro* (Georgia) newsletter

WANT TO GET HIGHER GRADES? READ

THE IDEA
To promote the fact that reading can increase students' grade point average.

THE MATERIALS: Cover the board with colorful paper or fabric. On large sheets of rectangular paper write each word in the caption "Want to Get Higher Grades? Read." Place the words on the board, with each one higher than the previous one. The last word, "Read," could be either at the top of the bulletin board or totally off the board, placed on the wall.

WHAT CAN YOU DO?

THE IDEA
To promote recycling among the students and staff.

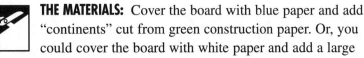

THE MATERIALS: Cover the board with blue paper and add "continents" cut from green construction paper. Or, you could cover the board with white paper and add a large paper earth at the bottom. Add the caption "What can you do?" List facts to encourage recycling and attach jackets from books that focus on this topic. The facts list could include:

- If the Pilgrims had used aluminum cans at the first Thanksgiving, the cans would still be around today.
- The average American spends eight full months of her life opening junk mail.
- In the United States, we throw away more than two million plastic bottles every hour.
- The ink of plastic bags contains cadmium, a toxic metal.

What you can do:

- Buy long-lasting, fuel-efficient tires. More than 240 million tires are discarded every year in the United States.
- If 100,000 people stopped their junk mail, we could save 150,000 trees every year.
- Turn the water off while you brush your teeth. This will save more than five gallons of water.

WHAT TEACHER HAS HAD THE MOST IMPACT ON YOU?

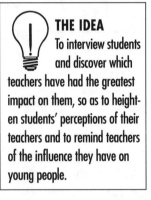

THE IDEA
To interview students and discover which teachers have had the greatest impact on them, so as to heighten students' perceptions of their teachers and to remind teachers of the influence they have on young people.

THE MATERIALS: Cover the bulletin board with black fabric or paper, to resemble a chalkboard. Using yellow paper or fabric, add the caption "What Teacher Has Had the Most Impact on You?" Interview students who visit the media center; ask them which teacher(s) has made a difference in their lives. Place their statements on the board. You may want to add the students' and teachers' pictures beside the testimonials.

Idea suggested by Felecia Spicer, Cotton Indian Elementary School, Stockbridge, Georgia

WHAT'S NEW?

THE IDEA
To promote reading with an eye-catching bulletin board.

THE MATERIALS: Cover the bulletin board with book jackets, then cover the board, jackets and all, with newspaper. Tear the newspaper so that it looks like the background is bursting through. In bright letters add the caption "What's New?"

Idea suggested by Leslie Pratschler, M. D. Roberts Middle School, Jonesboro, Georgia

WHATEVER

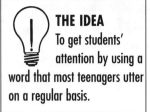

THE IDEA
To get students' attention by using a word that most teenagers utter on a regular basis.

THE MATERIALS: Cover the board with colorful fabric or paper and spell out "Whatever" in very large letters. In smaller letters, underneath, write, "you want to read… we have it." Surround the board with book jackets from your collection.

A WINNING COMBINATION: YOU AND YOUR MEDIA CENTER

THE IDEA
To show students that the library media center is a vital part of their high school education and a wonderful resource for learning and enjoyment.

THE MATERIALS: Cover the bulletin board with colorful paper. Place a large drawing of a school locker in the center of the board and add an extremely large combination lock on the locker door. The locker can be steel gray or a school color. Add details such as vents, locker number, etc. You could make the locker three-dimensional and have the door open. Add the caption "A Winning Combination: You and Your Media Center" and some appealing book jackets. Position one of the jackets so that it is sticking out from the locker door.

YOUR CAR NEEDS FUEL, SO DOES YOUR BRAIN

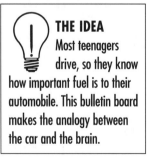

THE IDEA
Most teenagers drive, so they know how important fuel is to their automobile. This bulletin board makes the analogy between the car and the brain.

THE MATERIALS: Cover the bulletin board with blue fabric or paper. Add a cutout of a steering wheel and a cutout of a fuel gauge above the wheel. The gauge's needle should point toward "empty." Place a drawing of a library building in the distance. Add the caption "Your car needs fuel, so does your brain."

Catchy Captions

THE BOOK

THE IDEA

To remind students and staff that no matter how many computers the school owns or how much technology we have, the printed word is still a vital part of our lives.

THE MATERIALS: A wonderful background for this bulletin board is the American Library Association™ gift-wrapping paper, which is covered with the word "book" written in many different languages. Using the script below, put several sentences on individual sheets of paper and position the sheets of paper on the board.

The Book

Announcing the new, built-in, orderly, organized, knowledge device called… THE BOOK.

The BOOK is a revolutionary breakthrough in technology—no wires, no electrical circuits, no batteries, nothing to connect or switch on. It's so easy to use that even a child can operate it—just lift its cover! Compact and portable, it can be used anywhere—even sitting in an armchair by the fire—yet it's powerful enough to hold as much information as a CD-ROM.

Here's how it works.

Each BOOK is constructed of sequentially numbered sheets of paper, each of which is capable of holding thousands of bits of information. These pages are locked together with a custom-fit device, called a binder, that keeps the sheets in their correct sequence. OPT, or opaque paper technology, allows manufacturers to use both sides of the sheets, doubling the information density and cutting costs in half.

Each sheet is scanned optically, registering information directly into your brain. A flick of the finger takes you to the next sheet. The BOOK may be taken up at any time and used by merely opening it. The BOOK never crashes and never needs rebooting, though, like other display devices, it can become unusable if dropped overboard. The "browse" feature allows you to move instantly to any sheet and to move forward or backward as you wish. Many come with an "index" feature, which pinpoints the exact location of any selected information for instant retrieval.

An optional "bookmark" accessory allows you to open the BOOK to the exact place you left it in a previous session—even if the book has been closed. Bookmarks fit universal design standards; thus, a single bookmark can be used in BOOKs made by various manufacturers. Conversely, numerous bookmarkers can be used in a single BOOK, if the user wants to store numerous views at once. The number is limited only by the amount of pages in the BOOK.

You can also make personal notes next to BOOK text entries with an optional programming tool called the Portable Erasable Nib Cryptic Intercommunication Lance, commonly known as the pencil!

Portable, durable, and affordable, the BOOK is being hailed as the entertainment wave of the future.

–*Author unknown*

READING EACH DAY KEEPS THE F's AWAY

THE IDEA
To encourage students to use the library media center, check out books, and read them, to improve their grades.

THE MATERIALS: Cover the bulletin board with black or green paper, to resemble a chalkboard. The caption, "Reading Each Day Keeps the F's Away," should be prominently displayed. Survey honor roll students to find out how many books they check out from the library media center, then post the survey results. Imaginary "report cards" could be scattered around the board. Pictures of honor roll students reading, or quotes from the students explaining why they enjoy reading, also could be displayed. Attach jackets of various types of reading materials or books about study skills.

CAN YOU READ THIS?

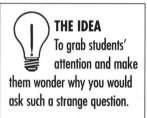

THE IDEA
To grab students' attention and make them wonder why you would ask such a strange question.

THE MATERIALS: Cover the bulletin board with bright, eye-catching colors to grab students' attention. Add the caption "Can You Read This?" The caption should be visually appealing, large enough to dominate the board, and centered in the board. Directly under the caption, in smaller print, add, "Then use that ability. Check out a book." Add book jackets and/or pictures of students checking out materials from the library media center.

CLASSIC PARK, WHERE LITERARY DINOSAURS COME TO LIFE

THE IDEA
To spotlight classic literature and dig up a little dinosaur interest at the same time.

THE MATERIALS: Cover the bulletin board with white paper. Have student artists create a large dinosaur head and upper body or use your opaque projector to create one. Place the dinosaur in the center of the board and, using red and black letters, write "Classic Park" directly on it. At the bottom of the bulletin board add, "Where literary dinosaurs come to life." Add book jackets or covers of timeless titles, whether they are required reading or simply overlooked classics from the past.
    See appendix for an example of this bulletin board. (Chart M)

Idea suggested by Brenda Stafford, Chesapeake, Virginia

DETERMINE YOUR PRIORITIES

THE IDEA
To convince students of the value of reading books.

THE MATERIALS: Cover the board with green paper. Add the caption "Determine Your Priorities." Add a few dollar signs or play money around the board. On a large, white sheet of paper list the following:

- New shoes: $100.00
- Prom dress: $300.00
- New CD: $15.00
- Gas for car: $10.00
- Reading a good book: Priceless

You can adapt the list to fit your student's priorities and likes.

EXERCISE YOUR RIGHT TO READ

THE IDEA
To encourage students and staff to exercise their right to read and to vote.

THE MATERIALS: Cover the bulletin board with large strips of red, white, and blue paper. Add the caption "Exercise Your Right to Read." Make political signs that read, "Vote Read." This board is appropriate any time, but especially during political campaigns. Add slogans such as "A Book in Every Book Bag," "I Like Reading," and "Vote for Reading."

FIRST YOU LEARNED TO READ, NOW READ TO LEARN

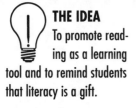

THE IDEA
To promote reading as a learning tool and to remind students that literacy is a gift.

THE MATERIALS: Cover the bulletin board with colorful paper. Add the caption "First You Learned to Read, Now Read to Learn." On one side of the board, place a picture or drawing of a young child reading and, on the other side, show a teenager reading. Add book jackets for color and interest.

FRIENDS DON'T LET FRIENDS READ JUNK

THE IDEA Use common or famous slogans to create an attention-getting bulletin board. For instance, the remark "Friends don't let friends drive drunk" is familiar to students, so change it a bit to encourage students to read classics and significant literature.

THE MATERIALS: Cover your bulletin board in an eye-catching color. Add the caption "Friends Don't Let Friends Read Junk." Take several pictures of friends reading and place the photos on the board. Surround the pictures with jackets from classics or from books on the school reading lists.

GET YOUR HEART RATE GOING—READ ONE OF THESE

THE IDEA To spotlight strange, frightening, and mysterious books.

THE MATERIALS: Cover the bulletin board with white paper. Add the caption "Get your heart rate going" at the top of the board and the caption "Read one of these" at the bottom. Include a red, zigzag, "heart monitor" line across the center. Scatter theme-appropriate book titles or jackets around the board, such as *Frankenstein, Jaws, Dracula,* and *Jurassic Park,* or titles by Edgar Allan Poe, Lois Duncan, Agatha Christie, and Stephen King.

Idea suggested by Maggie Serritella, Student, State University of West Georgia

HURRY

THE IDEA To encourage reading by making a succinct point. A small sign in the middle of the board tells students how many books are in the library media center and how many students/patrons the library serves, then offers a word of advice.

THE MATERIALS: Cover the bulletin board with a bright color. In the center of the board place a small sign that reads:

> 17,000 books
>
> 2,300 students
>
> Hurry

(The numbers should reflect your school and library media center.)

IF YOU START HERE, YOU CAN GO ANYWHERE

THE IDEA
This caption shows students that the library media center is a vital part of their lives that can have an important and positive impact on them.

THE MATERIALS: Cover the bulletin board with colorful material. Add the caption "If You Start Here, You Can Go Anywhere." Create a game-board effect by arranging squares of different colors to resemble a chess or checkers board. Each square contains a message such as "You read *Treasure Island*. Move ahead 3 squares" or "You learned to use an almanac. Move ahead 1 square." The last square should read, "Your future. Keep using your library."

JUST THE FACTS, MA'AM

THE IDEA
To promote books that are primarily concerned with facts, such as almanacs, books of lists, world record books, sports books, etc.

THE MATERIALS: Cover the bulletin board with colorful paper. Create the upper body of a police officer from paper and place it in the center of the board. Position a dialogue "bubble" above the officer's head and write, "Just the facts, ma'am" in it. Surround the officer with jackets of books from your library media center that focus on facts.

KNOWLEDGE IS POWER

THE IDEA
To let students know that their library media center is a place of power.

THE MATERIALS: Cover the bulletin board with colorful fabric or paper. Add the caption "Knowledge Is Power." Draw a weight lifter lifting a barbell. Cut a page copied from a dictionary or a book jacket into circles and attach them to the ends of the barbells as "weights," so that it looks as if the weight lifter is "pumping" knowledge.

LIKE HAVING A CHOICE? THE LIBRARY MEDIA CENTER HAS 16,000 CHOICES

THE IDEA To let your students and faculty know that they have many choices when they enter your library media center. (The number in the caption should reflect the number of items in your collection.)

THE MATERIALS: Cover the board with colorful fabric or paper. The caption is the whole theme, so make it large and interesting.

A POSTCARD FROM THE LIBRARY MEDIA CENTER

THE IDEA To promote the library media center as a retreat for students and staff.

THE MATERIALS: Cover the board with blue paper. Add the caption "A Postcard from the Library Media Center." On a large sheet of white paper create a "postcard." On the right side of the card draw a stamp and address the card to the *Students at [Your] School*. On the left side write, *"Wish you were here,"* and sign it from the library media staff. Attach the "postcard" at an angle on the bulletin board. You can add jackets of books about vacation spots or let the board speak for itself.

QUIT YOUR WHINING!

THE IDEA To help teenagers, who sometimes dwell on the negative, change their focus to a more positive one.

THE MATERIALS: Cover the board with black paper. Using a bright color add the caption "Quit your whining!" Find biographies in your collection that concentrate on people who have overcome adversity, health problems, physical handicaps, or poverty. Add titles or jackets of books that are appropriate to this category. You could focus on the following people or think of your own examples:

- Franklin Roosevelt
- Ulysses S. Grant
- Scott Hamilton
- Stevie Wonder
- Helen Keller
- Stephen Hawking
- Lance Armstrong

READ FOR A LIFETIME...MAYBE LONGER

THE IDEA
To celebrate the Halloween season and focus on a lifetime of reading.

THE MATERIALS: Cover the bulletin board with black paper. Add the caption "Read for a Lifetime… Maybe Longer" in orange or yellow letters. Place a skeleton figure in the center of the board. (The pose-able skeleton figures sold during Halloween are perfect for this.) Place a book jacket in the skeleton's hands and other jackets around the board.

READ _{FOR} YOUR MIND

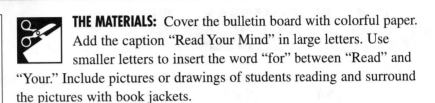

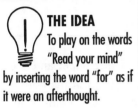

THE IDEA
To play on the words "Read your mind" by inserting the word "for" as if it were an afterthought.

THE MATERIALS: Cover the bulletin board with colorful paper. Add the caption "Read Your Mind" in large letters. Use smaller letters to insert the word "for" between "Read" and "Your." Include pictures or drawings of students reading and surround the pictures with book jackets.

SCHOOL BORED? TRY THESE

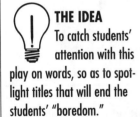

THE IDEA
To catch students' attention with this play on words, so as to spotlight titles that will end the students' "boredom."

THE MATERIALS: Cover the board with bright paper or fabric. Place the caption "School Bored?" at the top of the board and the subtitle "Try These" at the bottom. Add book jackets that definitely are *not* boring.

SLIP INTO THESE OLD FAVORITES

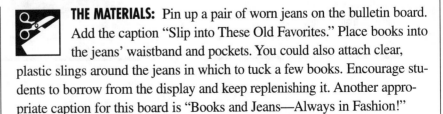

THE IDEA
To focus attention on classics and older novels that the students may not have read.

THE MATERIALS: Pin up a pair of worn jeans on the bulletin board. Add the caption "Slip into These Old Favorites." Place books into the jeans' waistband and pockets. You could also attach clear, plastic slings around the jeans in which to tuck a few books. Encourage students to borrow from the display and keep replenishing it. Another appropriate caption for this board is "Books and Jeans—Always in Fashion!"

Idea suggested by Sharon Cataldo, Kelso State School, Kelso Qld, Australia

THE TRUTH IS IN HERE...COME IN AND CHECK IT OUT

THE IDEA
To encourage students to come to the media center. This caption works especially well if your clientele enjoys science fiction, but it will succeed even if they do not recognize the slogan.

THE MATERIALS: Cover the bulletin board with black fabric or paper. Or, you could use a fabric with an outer-space theme. In large letters add the caption "The Truth Is in Here." If your bulletin board is outside of the library media center, you may want to write "The Truth Is in There," accompanied by an arrow pointing toward the library media center. Add book jackets or covers that deal with science fiction or use the caption to focus on nonfiction materials.

THERE'S NO PLACE LIKE TOME

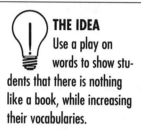

THE IDEA
Use a play on words to show students that there is nothing like a book, while increasing their vocabularies.

THE MATERIALS: Cover the board with white paper and add the caption "There's No Place like Tome!" Cut out the bottom of a blue dress from construction paper, and add a pair of legs that end in feet wearing ruby slippers. Add jackets of books that deal with fantasy or any other topic you wish to highlight.

THESE BOOKS WILL KEEP YOU AWAKE!

THE IDEA
To promote frightening books. Many students and faculty love to read mystery, fantasy, or horror books. This bulletin board should grab their attention.

THE MATERIALS: Cover the background with black fabric or paper. Cut two large, white, oval shapes to look like eyes. Cut smaller black circles for the pupils. The caption should read "These Books Will Keep You Awake!" Surround the "eyes" with book jackets from appropriately scary titles.

THESE BOOKS WILL KNOCK YOUR SOCKS OFF!

THE IDEA
To promote books that are frightening, mysterious, weird, and worrisome. Teenagers flock to movies that keep them on the edge of their seat, so publicize books that will make them afraid to turn the page.

THE MATERIALS: Cover your bulletin board with a color of your choosing. Add the caption "These Books Will Knock Your Socks Off!" Hang real socks on the board. (You can ask your faculty and staff to contribute to the sock fund.) Surround the socks with jackets from some of your scarier titles. You also could use a skeleton in the background.

THINGS ARE LOOKING UP AT THE LIBRARY MEDIA CENTER

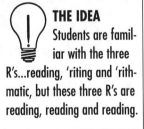

THE IDEA
To promote the library media center and publicize books that focus on feeling good about yourself.

THE MATERIALS: Cover the bulletin board with colorful paper. Add the caption "Things Are Looking Up at the Library Media Center." Draw two extra-large eyes on white paper, placing black pupils at the top of them. Attach construction-paper eyelashes to give the eyes a three-dimensional look. Spotlight books on self-esteem, self-confidence, and self-assurance.

See appendix for an example of this bulletin board. (Chart A)

DON'T FORGET THE THREE R's: READ, READ, READ

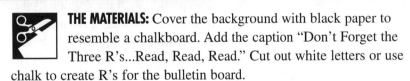

THE IDEA
Students are familiar with the three R's...reading, 'riting and 'rithmatic, but these three R's are reading, reading and reading.

THE MATERIALS: Cover the background with black paper to resemble a chalkboard. Add the caption "Don't Forget the Three R's...Read, Read, Read." Cut out white letters or use chalk to create R's for the bulletin board.

WE'RE THE TALK OF THE SCHOOL

THE IDEA
To promote the library media center by using pictures of students and teachers, and their comments about the library, its staff, its services, and its materials.

THE MATERIALS: Cover the bulletin board with colorful paper or fabric. Add the word "Library" in very large letters that cover the width of the board. Take digital photos of students and staff and place them on the board. Add their comments in dialogue "bubbles" above their heads.

Idea suggested by Nancy Garabed, LMS, Council Rock High School, Newtown, Pennsylvania

WANT THE WHOLE STORY?

THE IDEA
Everyone wants to know the whole story: the entire plot and all of the facts.

THE MATERIALS: Cover the bulletin board with a colorful fabric or paper. Add the caption "Want the Whole Story?" and a large drawing of a closed book. Include an arrow pointing to the pages and the caption "Open here."

WHAT'S COOKING AT OUR SCHOOL?

THE IDEA
To spotlight Home Economics students and/or cafeteria workers. A lot of students who participate in cooking classes would be delighted to see themselves featured on the bulletin board. And, many students eat lunch at school, but do not know the staff that prepares the food.

THE MATERIALS: Cover the board with colorful fabric or paper. (You could use fabric with a kitchen or food theme as a background.) Add the caption "What's Cooking at Our School?" Take pictures of students in Home Economics class and/or of cafeteria workers preparing lunch, then post them on the board. Include cookbook jackets or pictures of cookbooks from the library media center. Try adding international cookbooks or a recipe or two to make an interesting board for students to savor.

YOU ARE IN MY POWER

THE IDEA
To create the illusion of hypnotizing students and asking them to come into the library media center.

THE MATERIALS: Create a large, circular pattern of alternating red and white spirals on the bulletin board (it should take up most of the board). In the center of the pattern write the caption "You Are in My Power—Come to the Library Media Center." Add jackets of books about hypnosis, psychology, or a subject of your choosing.

YOUR MOM CALLED

THE IDEA
To suggest that even moms think students should use the library media center.

THE MATERIALS: Cover the bulletin board with colorful paper. Add the caption "Your mom called. She said to read a book!" Draw a cartoon of a mother talking to her child on the telephone. Place a large telephone receiver between the mother and student and attach telephone cords going in both directions. Add book jackets that even a mother could love.

WHICH WAY? KNOW WAY!

THE IDEA
Use a catchy slogan to show students that the library media center is the way to know things.

THE MATERIALS: Cover the bulletin board with black fabric or paper to resemble a street or road. Using materials reminiscent of local street signs, create a double street sign. One sign should read, "Which Way?" and the other should read, "Know Way!" If your bulletin board is outside of the library media center, position the "Know Way" sign to point toward the center's doors. Fill the remaining space with book covers from reference books and nonfiction materials.

WHO'S WHO AND WHAT'S WHAT

THE IDEA
To encourage students to stay abreast of current events and people in the news by promoting your periodicals and newspapers.

THE MATERIALS: Cover your bulletin board with newspaper. Add a red border for a splash of color. The caption, "Who's Who and What's What," can also be in red, or in black. Add names of people currently in the news, copies of newsmagazine covers, and pictures of important events or of world leaders. This board can be either informative or interactive. To make it informative, simply list the information. To make it interactive, have students try to determine who the noteworthy people are.

Literary Quotations

QUOTATIONS ABOUT LIBRARIES, LIBRARIANS, BOOKS, AND READING

Mortimer Jerome Adler: In the case of good books, the point is not to see how many of them you can get through, but rather how many can get through to you.

Mortimer Jerome Adler: Reading is a basic tool in the living of a good life.

Louisa May Alcott: Some books are so familiar that reading them is like being home again.

Richard Armour: Library: Here is where people, one frequently finds, lower their voices, and raise their minds.

Arthur Ashe: Throughout my formal education I spent many, many hours in public and school libraries. Libraries became courts of last resort, as it were. The current definitive answer to almost any question can be found within the four walls of most libraries.

Francis Bacon: Some books are to be tasted, others to be swallowed, and some few to be chewed and digested.

Henry Ward Beecher: Books are not made for furniture, but there is nothing else that so beautifully furnishes a house.

Henry Ward Beecher: A book is a garden, an orchard, a storehouse, a party, a company by the way, a counselor, a multitude of counselors.

Stephen Vincent Benet: Books are not men and yet they stay alive.

Bernard Berenson: My house is a library with living rooms attached.

Jorge Luis Borges: I have always imagined that Paradise will be a kind of library.

Jorge Luis Borges: I have always come to life after coming to books.

Ray Bradbury: You must live feverishly in a library. Colleges are not going to do any good unless you are raised and live in a library every day of your life.

Ray Bradbury: You don't have to burn books to destroy a culture. Just get people to stop reading them.

Ray Bradbury: Without libraries what have we? We have no past and no future.

Joseph Brodsky: There are worse crimes than burning books. One of them is not reading them.

Elizabeth Barrett Browning: Books, books, books had found the secret of a garret-room piled high with cases in my father's name; Piled high, packed large, where, creeping in and out among the giant fossils of my past, like some small nimble mouse between the ribs of a mastodon, I nibbled here and there at this or that box, pulling through the gap, in heats of terror, haste, victorious joy, the first book first. And how I felt it beat under my pillow, in the morning's dark. An hour before the sun would let me read! My books!

Edmund Burke: To read without reflecting is like eating without digesting.

Thomas Carlyle: The true University of these days is a collection of books.

Andrew Carnegie: There is not such a cradle of democracy upon the earth as the Free Public Library, this republic of letters, where neither rank, office, nor wealth receives the slightest consideration.

Chinese proverb: A book is like a garden carried in the pocket.

Rufus Choate: A book is the only immortality.

Cicero: Anyone who has a library and a garden wants for nothing.

Cicero: A room without books is like a body without a soul.

Samuel Taylor Coleridge: Force yourself to reflect on what you read, paragraph by paragraph.

Samuel Taylor Coleridge: Readers may be divided into four classes: 1. Sponges, who absorb all that they read and return it in nearly the same state, only a little dirtied. 2. Sand glasses, who retain nothing and are content to get through a book for the sake of getting through the time. 3. Strain-bags, who retain merely the dregs of what they read. 4. Mogul diamonds, equally rare and valuable, who profit by what they read, and enable others to profit by it also.

Jeremy Collier: Books support us in our solitude and keep us from being a burden to ourselves.

Henry Steele Commager: Censorship always defeats its own purpose, for it creates in the end the kind of society that is incapable of exercising real discretion.

Norman Cousins: The library should be the delivery room for the birth of ideas—a place where history comes to life.

Walter Cronkite: Whatever the cost of our libraries, the price is cheap compared to that of an ignorant nation.

Emily Dickinson: There is no frigate like a book to take us lands away, nor any coursers like a page of prancing poetry.

Kirk Douglas: My mother and father were illiterate immigrants from Russia. When I was a child they were constantly amazed that could go to a building and take a book on any subject. They couldn't believe this access to knowledge we have here in America. They couldn't believe that it was free.

Arthur Conan Doyle: It is a great thing to start life with a small number of really good books which are your very own.

Clyde Edgerton: Librarians are at the heart of opposition to foolish, dangerous, misguided attempts at censoring human expression in our free country. I thank God for their efforts.

Ralph Waldo Emerson: What's a book? Everything or nothing. The eye that sees it all.

Ralph Waldo Emerson: Books are to inspire.

Ralph Waldo Emerson: If we encounter a man of rare intellect, we should ask him what books he reads.

Ralph Waldo Emerson: In a library we are surrounded by many hundreds of dear friends imprisoned by an enchanter in paper and leathern boxes.

Ralph Waldo Emerson: 'Tis the good reader that makes the good book.

Gloria Estefan: The part of my education that has had the deepest influence wasn't any particular essay or even a specific class; it was how I was able to apply everything I learned in the library to certain situations in my life.

Helen Exley: Books can be dangerous. The best ones should be labeled, "This could change your life."

Clifton Fadiman: When you read a classic you do not see in the book more than you did before. You see more in you than there was before.

Jim Fiebig: There is a wonder in reading Braille that the sighted will never know: to touch words and have them touch you back.

Gustave Flaubert: Read in order to live.

Malcolm Forbes: The richest person in the world—in fact all the riches in the world—couldn't provide you with anything like the endless, incredible loot available at your local library. You can measure the awareness, the breadth, and the wisdom of a civilization, a nation, a people, by the priority given to preserving these repositories of all that we are, all that we were, or will be.

Jean Fritz: When I discovered libraries, it was like having Christmas every day.

William Ewart Gladstone: Books are delightful society. If you go into a room and find it full of books—even without taking them from the shelves they seem to speak to you, to bid you welcome.

Sue Grafton: A library is the world at your fingertips.

Germaine Greer: Libraries are reservoirs of strength, grace and wit, reminders of order, calm and continuity, lakes of mental energy, neither warm nor cold, light or dark. The pleasure they give us is steady, unorgastic, reliable, deep and long lasting. In any library in the world, I am home, unselfconscious, still, and absorbed.

Alex Haley: My parents were teachers and they went out of their way to see to it that I had books. We grew up in a home that was full of books. And so I learned to read. I loved to read.

Elizabeth Hamilton: It is only by the love of reading that the evil resulting from the association with little minds can be counteracted.

S. I. Hayakawa: In a very real sense, people who have read good literature have lived more than people who cannot or will not read.

Katharine Hepburn: What in the world would we do without our libraries?

Anne Herbert: Libraries will get you through times of no money better than money will get you through times of no libraries.

Alice Hoffman: Books may well be the only true magic.

Harold Howe, former United States Commissioner of Education: What a school thinks about its library is a measure of what it thinks about education.

Aldous Huxley: The proper study of mankind is books.

Thomas Jefferson: I cannot live without books.

Thomas Jefferson: Books constitute capital.

Lady Bird Johnson: Perhaps no place in any community is so totally democratic as the town library. The only entrance requirement is interest.

Franz Kafka: A book must be an ice axe to break the seas frozen inside our soul.

Jan Karon: A library is home to one of my favorite things: Librarians.

Helen Keller: Literature is my Utopia.

John Kieran: I am a part of everything that I have read.

Juliana Kimball: The libraries have become my candy store.

Barbara Kingsolver: I'm of a fearsome mind to throw my arms around every living librarian who crosses my path, on behalf of the souls they never knew they saved.

Louis L'Amour: For one who reads, there is no limit to the number of lives that may be lived, for fiction, biography, and history offer an inexhaustible number of lives in many parts of the world, in all periods of time.

Keith Curry Lance: Students who score higher on tests tend to come from schools which have more library resource staff and more books, periodicals, and videos, and where the instructional role of the teacher-librarian and involvement in cooperative program planning and teaching is more prominent.

Harper Lee: Until I feared I would lose it, I never loved to read. One does not love breathing.

Julius Lester: A library is the place where wonder lives.

C. S. Lewis: We read to know we are not alone.

Abraham Lincoln: Books serve to show a man that those original thoughts of his aren't very new after all.

Henry Wadsworth Longfellow: The love of learning, the sequestered nooks, and all the sweet serenity of books.

Lord Edward Lytton: In science, read by preference the newest works. In literature, read the oldest. The classics are always modern.

David McCullough: We must not think of learning as only what happens in schools. It is an extended part of life. The most readily available resource for all of life is our public library system.

Archibald MacLeish: What is more important in a library than anything else—than everything else—is the fact that it exists.

Maimonides: Do not consider it proof just because it is written in books, for a liar who will deceive with his tongue will not hesitate to do the same with his pen.

Heinrich Mann: A house without books is like a room without windows. No man has a right to bring up children without surrounding them with books. Children learn to read being in the presence of books.

Horace Mann: Resolve to edge in a little reading every day, if it is but a single sentence. If you gain 15 minutes a day, it will make itself felt at the end of the year.

Katherine Mansfield: The pleasure of reading is doubled when one lives with another who shares the same books.

M. Somerset Maugham: To acquire the habit of reading is to construct for yourself a refuge from almost all of the miseries of life.

M. Somerset Maugham: The only important thing in a book is the meaning it has for you.

Groucho Marx: Outside of a dog, a book is man's best friend. Inside a dog, it's too dark to read.

James McCosh: The book to read is not the one which thinks for you, but the one which makes you think.

Henry Miller: We should read to give our souls a chance to luxuriate.

John Milton: He who destroys a good book kills reason itself.

Robert Morgan: A library is richer than Fort Knox and everyone has the key.

Toni Morrison: If there's a book you really want to read but it hasn't been written yet, then you must write it.

Kathleen Norris: Just the knowledge that a good book is waiting for one at the end of a long day makes that day happier.

Katherine Paterson: A library is a feast to which we're all invited.

Richard Peck: A library is every young reader's ticket out of town.

Regis Philbin: What can I say? Librarians rule.

Franklin Delano Roosevelt: People die, but books never die.

Roger Rosenblatt: A library should be like a pair of open arms.

J. D. Salinger: What really knocks me out is a book that, when you're all done reading it, you wish the author that wrote it was a terrific friend of yours.

Willard Scott: Librarians have always been among the most thoughtful and helpful people. They are teachers without a classroom. No libraries, no progress.

Dr. Seuss: The more that you read, the more things you will know. The more that you learn, the more places you'll go.

Percy Bysshe Shelley: Poets are the unacknowledged legislators of the world.

B. F. Skinner: We shouldn't teach great books; we should teach a love of reading.

Richard Steele: Reading is to the mind what exercise is to the body. It is wholesome and bracing for the mind to have its faculties kept on the stretch. (This quote is also attributed to Joseph Addison, who was a contemporary of Steele's.)

William Styron: A great book should leave you with many experiences, and slightly exhausted. You should live several lives while reading it.

Henry David Thoreau: How many a man has dated a new era in his life from the reading of a book.

Mark Twain: The man who does not read good books has no advantage over the man that cannot read them.

H. G. Wells: I had just taken to reading. I had just discovered the art of leaving my body to sit impassive in a crumpled up attitude in a chair or sofa, while I wandered over the hills and far way in novel company and new scenes…. My world began to expand very rapidly, the reading habit had got me securely.

H. G. Wells: Good books are the warehouses of ideas.

Oscar Wilde: There is no such thing as a moral or an immoral book. Books are well written, or badly written.

Oscar Wilde: It is what you read when you don't have to that determines what you will be when you can't help it.

Bern Williams: Books had instant replay long before televised sports.

William Carlos Williams: A cool of books will sometimes lead the mind to libraries of a hot afternoon, if books can be found cool to the sense to lead the mind away.

Virginia Woolf: I ransack public libraries, and find them full of sunk treasure.

Christopher Wren: Choose an author as you choose a friend.

Malcolm X: I have often reflected upon the new vistas that reading opened to me. I knew right there in prison that reading had changed forever the course of my life. As I see it today, the ability to read awoke in me some long dormant craving to be mentally alive.

Malcolm X: My alma mater was books, a good library.

Appendix

January

SUNDAY	MONDAY	TUESDAY	WEDNESDAY	THURSDAY	FRIDAY	SATURDAY
1 J. D. Salinger born: 1919	**2** Birthday of Issac Asimov: 1920	**3** J. R. R. Tolkein born: 1892	**4** Jacob Grimm born: 1785	**5** George W. Carver died in 1943. In 1945 Congress declared Jan. 5 as George Washington Carver Day	**6** Carl Sandburg born: 1878	**7** 1st photograph of genes: 1949
8 1st telegraph message transmitted: 1838	**9** Concorde tested: 1969	**10** Thomas Paine published *Common Sense*: 1776	**11** Element 87 (Francium) announced: 1930	**12** Jack London born: 1976	**13** James Joyce died: 1941	**14** Birthday of Hugh Lofting: 1886
15 Martin Luther King Jr. born: 1929	**16** Remains of 7,000-year-old mastadon found: 1962	**17** Robert Cormier born: 1925 Ben Franklin born: 1706	**18** Birthday of A. A. Milne: 1882	**19** Birthday of Edgar Allan Poe: 1809	**20** Birthday of Leadbelly: 1889	**21** Traffic light invented: 1923
22 Lord Byron born: 1788 Birthday of Joseph Wambaugh	**23** Graduation of 1st woman physician, Elizabeth Blackwell: 1849	**24** Birthday of Edith Wharton: 1862	**25** Robert Burns born: 1759 W. Somerset Maugham born: 1874	**26** Electric dental drill patented: 1875	**27** Lewis Caroll born: 1832 Mozart born: 1756	**28** Challenger Space Shuttle explosion: 1986
29 Thomas Paine and William McKinley born	**30** Library of Congress purchased Jefferson's library: 1815	**31** Truman orders development of H-bomb: 1950 Norman Mailer born: 1923	**JANUARY IS MARCH OF DIMES DEFECTS PREVENTION MONTH.**	**JANUARY IS NATIONAL HOBBY MONTH.**	**JANUARY ALSO HOSTS SCHOOL NURSE DAY.**	

February

SUNDAY	MONDAY	TUESDAY	WEDNESDAY	THURSDAY	FRIDAY	SATURDAY
1 Langston Hughes born: 1902	**2** Birthday of James Joyce: 1882	**3** Sidney Lanier born: 1834	**4** Charles Lindbergh born: 1902	**5** Birthday of Hank Aaron: 1934	**6** Babe Ruth's birthday: 1895	**7** Birthday of Charles Dickens: 1812
8 Boy Scouts founded: 1910	**9** Weather Bureau authorized: 1870	**10** 1st singing telegram: 1933	**11** Thomas Edison born: 1847	**12** Birthday of Abe Lincoln: 1809	**13** 1st public school: 1635	**14** Valentine's Day
15 Birthday of Galileo, Cyrus McCormick & Susan B. Anthony	**16** Nylon patented: 1937	**17** Postal Service established: 1691	**18** 9th planet discovered:1930 Toni Morrison born: 1931	**19** Marines invade Iwo Jima: 1945 Carson McCullers born: 1917	**20** John Glenn orbits the earth: 1962	**21** Last green-and-yellow Carolina parakeet died: 1918
22 Birthday of George Washington: 1732	**23** 1st use of Salk vaccine: 1954	**24** President Johnson impeached: 1868	**25** 1st African-American congressman sworn in: 1870	**26** World Trade Center bombed: 1993	**27** Birthday of Henry W. Longfellow: 1807 John Steinbeck born: 1902	**28** Republican Party began: 1854
29 1st African-American woman to win an Oscar: 1940	**FEBRUARY IS BLACK HISTORY MONTH.**	**FEBRUARY IS LIBRARY LOVERS MONTH.**	**FEBRUARY IS AMERICAN HEART MONTH.**			

March

SUNDAY	MONDAY	TUESDAY	WEDNESDAY	THURSDAY	FRIDAY	SATURDAY
1 1st census: 1790 Salem Witch trials begin: 1692	**2** Dr. Seuss' birthday! (1904)	**3** *Star Spangled Banner* declared National Anthem: 1931	**4** Jane Godall's birthday: 1934	**5** Birthday of William Steinway: 1797	**6** Ring Lardner, Michelangelo, and Elizabeth Barrett Browning born	**7** Telephone patented: 1876
8 Birthday of Oliver Wendell Holmes, Jr.: 1841	**9** Amerigo Vespucci born: 1454	**10** Death of Harriet Tubman: 1913 James Herriott born:	**11** 1st Hindu woman receives medical degree, Anandibai Joshee: 1886	**12** Juliette Low founded Girl Scouts: 1912	**13** Uranus discovered: 1781	**14** Albert Einstein's birthday: 1879
15 Julius Caesar assassinated: 44 B.C.	**16** 1st black newspaper published: 1827	**17** Discovery of Element 98: 1950 St. Patrick's Day	**18** Grover Cleveland born: 1837 John Updike born: 1932	**19** Birthday of Phillip Roth: 1933	**20** *Uncle Tom's Cabin* published: 1852	**21** Birthday of Johann Bach: 1685
22 Randolph Caldecott born: 1846	**23** Patrick Henry gives famous speech: 1775	**24** 26th amendment ratified: 1971	**25** Birthday of Flannery O'Connor: 1925	**26** Birthday of Robert Frost (1874) & Tennessee Williams (1911)	**27** Alaskan earthquake: 1964	**28** Washing machine patented: 1707
29 Cy Young and John Tyler born	**30** Amendment 15 ratified: 1870 Birthday of Vincent van Gogh: 1853	**31** Eiffel Tower officially opened: 1889	**MARCH HAS READ ACROSS AMERICA DAY AND FREEDOM OF INFORMATION DAY.**	**MARCH IS WOMEN'S HISTORY MONTH AND YOUTH ART MONTH.**	**MUSCULAR DYSTROPHY SHAMROCK SALE.**	

April

SUNDAY	MONDAY	TUESDAY	WEDNESDAY	THURSDAY	FRIDAY	SATURDAY
1 Air Force Academy authorized: 1954	**2** Aluminum patented: 1889 Hans Christian Anderson born: 1805	**3** Washington Irving born: 1783	**4** Alexander Hamilton Appointed Postmaster General: 1692	**5** Booker T. Washington born: 1856	**6** Robert Peary and Matthew Henson reach the North Pole: 1909	**7** William Wordsworth born: 1770
8 1st 3-D movie shown: 1953	**9** Marian Anderson sings at Lincoln Memorial: 1939	**10** Clare Luce Booth born: 1903 Paul Theroux born: 1941	**11** Jackie Robinson becomes 1st black major league baseball player: 1947	**12** Fort Sumter attacked: 1861	**13** Birthday of Thomas Jefferson: 1743	**14** John Wilkes Booth shot Lincoln: 1865
15 Birthday of Leonardo da Vinci: 1452	**16** Wilbur Wright born: 1867	**17** Bay of Pigs Invasion: 1961	**18** Paul Revere's famous ride: 1775	**19** Revolutionary War begins: 1775	**20** Wisconsin Territory established: 1836	**21** Charlotte Bronte born: 1816
22 Henry Fielding born: 1707	**23** Birthday of William Shakespeare: 1564	**24** Library of Congress established: 1800	**25** 1st dogs trained to lead blind: 1928	**26** John James Audubon: 1785	**27** U. S. Grant born: 1822	**28** Birthday of Harper Lee and Lois Duncan:
29 1st college for blacks opened, Lincoln University: 1854	**30** Washington inaugurated: 1789 Louisiana Purchase: 1803	**APRIL IS SCHOOL LIBRARY MEDIA MONTH, AND NATIONAL LIBRARY WEEK.**	**APRIL IS CANCER PREVENTION MONTH.**	**APRIL HAS INTERNATIONAL CHILDREN'S BOOK DAY.**	**APRIL IS POETRY MONTH.**	

May

SUNDAY	MONDAY	TUESDAY	WEDNESDAY	THURSDAY	FRIDAY	SATURDAY
1 1st American climbs Mt. Everest: 1963	**2** Dr. Benjamin Spock born: 1902	**3** Battle of the Coral Sea begins (WWI): 1942	**4** Horace Mann born: 1796	**5** Cinco de Mayo: 1892	**6** Willie Mays born: 1931 Theodore White born: 1915	**7** Birthday of Robert Browning: 1812
8 Harry Truman born: 1884	**9** 1st political cartoon published in U.S.: 1754	**10** Mandela inaugurated as South African president: 1994	**11** Minnesota enters union: 1858	**12** Florence Nightingale born: 1820	**13** Jamestown founded: 1607	**14** Jenner administers 1st smallpox vaccine: 1796
15 L. Frank Baum born: 1856 Katherine Anne Porter born: 1894	**16** Elizabeth Peabody born: 1804	**17** Supreme Court rules in Brown v. Board of Education: 1954	**18** Mt. St. Helens erupts: 1980	**19** John Hopkins born: 1795	**20** *Spirit of St. Louis* leaves for nonstop flight: 1927	**21** Amelia Earhart completes Trans-Atlantic flight: 1932
22 Abe Lincoln receives patent: 1849 Authur Conan Doyle born: 1859	**23** 1st Kindergarten in United States: 1827	**24** Brooklyn Bridge opens: 1883	**25** Birthday of Ralph Waldo Emerson: 1803	**26** Montana Territory created: 1864 Birthday of Sally Ride: 1951	**27** Rachel Carson born: 1907 Dashiell Hammett born: 1894	**28** French and Indian War began: 1756 Ian Fleming born: 1908
29 Patrick Henry born: 1736 Wisconsin enters union: 1848	**30** Joan of Arc martyred: 1431	**31** Birthday of Walt Whitman: 1819	**MAY IS NATIONAL BOOK MONTH.**	**IT'S GET CAUGHT READING MONTH.**	**WORLD NO-TOBACCO DAY TAKES PLACE IN MAY.**	

June

SUNDAY	MONDAY	TUESDAY	WEDNESDAY	THURSDAY	FRIDAY	SATURDAY
1 John Mansfield born: 1878	**2** Thomas Hardy born: 1840	**3** DeSoto claims Florida for Spain: 1539	**4** Battle of Midway began: 1942	**5** Marshall Plan introduced: 1947	**6** Nathan Hale born: 1755 Thomas Mann born: 1875	**7** Gwendolyn Brooks born: 1917
8 Frank Lloyd Wright born: 1867	**9** Cole Porter born: 1893	**10** Birthday of Maurice Sendak: 1928	**11** John Quincy Adams born: 1767	**12** Anne Frank born: 1929	**13** Birthday of William Butler Yeats: 1865	**14** Harriet Beecher Stowe born: 1811
15 Arkansas enters union: 1836	**16** Ford Motor Company founded: 1903	**17** Birthday of John Hersey: 1914	**18** Birthday of Sylvia Porter: 1890	**19** Statue of Liberty arrived from France: 1885	**20** Lillian Hellman born: 1905 West Virginia becomes state: 1863	**21** Birthday of Rockwell Kent: 1882
22 Anne Morrow Lindbergh born: 1906	**23** Secret Service established: 1865	**24** Ambrose Bierce born: 1842	**25** Custer's Last Stand: 1876	**26** Birthday of Pearl S. Buck: 1892	**27** Paul L. Dunbar born: 1872 Helen Keller born: 1880	**28** World War I begins: 1914
29 George Goethals born: 1858	**30** Yosemite National Park established: 1864	**JUNE HAS FLAG DAY AND FATHER'S DAY.**	**JUNE IS NATIONAL SAFETY MONTH.**			

July

SUNDAY	MONDAY	TUESDAY	WEDNESDAY	THURSDAY	FRIDAY	SATURDAY
1 Battle of Gettysburg began: 1863 George Sand born: 1804	**2** President Garfield shot: 1881 Thurgood Marshall born: 1908	**3** Idaho became 43rd state: 1890 George M. Cohan born: 1878	**4** Calvin Coolidge born: 1872 Continental Congress adopted Declaration of Independence: 1776	**5** 26th Amendment passed: 1872 P. T. Barnham born: 1810	**6** Beatrix Potter born: 1866 Althea Gibson won at Wimbledon: 1957	**7** Birthday of Sherlock Holmes' sidekick, Dr. Watson: 1852 Satchel Paige born: 1906
8 "Boss Tweed" exposed by the *NY Times*: 1871	**9** Elias Howe born: 1819	**10** Mary McLeod Bethune born: 1875 Wyoming entered union: 1890	**11** John Quincy Adams born: 1767	**12** Henry David Thoreau born: 1817	**13** First television theater opens: 1938	**14** Gerald Ford born: 1913
15 Rembrandt born: 1606	**16** *Catcher in the Rye* published: 1951 District of Columbia established: 1790	**17** Postdam Conference convenes: 1945	**18** Nelson Mandela born: 1918 William Makepeace Thackeray born: 1811	**19** Edgar Degas born: 1834	**20** Neil Armstrong walks on the moon: 1969 Petrarch born: 1304	**21** Ernest Hemingway born: 1899
22 Stephan Vincent Benet born: 1898	**23** Typewriter patented in the United States: 1829	**24** Amelia Earhart born: 1897	**25** Puerto Rico becomes a common-wealth: 1952	**26** George Bernard Shaw born: 1856	**27** Gertrude Stein died: 1946	**28** Amendment 14 passed: 1868
29 Booth Tarkington born: 1869	**30** Henry Ford born: 1863 Emily Bronte born: 1818	**31**				

August

SUNDAY	MONDAY	TUESDAY	WEDNESDAY	THURSDAY	FRIDAY	SATURDAY
1 Herman Melville born: 1819 Colorado enters union: 1876	**2** Birthday of James Baldwin: 1924	**3** Christopher Columbus sets sail: 1492 P.D. James born: 1920	**4** Percy Shelley born: 1792	**5** Guy de Maupasssant born: 1850	**6** Alfred, Lord Tennyson born: 1809	**7** Ralph Bunche born: 1904
8 Sara Teasdale born: 1884 Birthday of Marjorie Kinnan Rawlings: 1896	**9** John Dryden born: 1631	**10** Missouri enters union: 1821 Herbert Hoover born: 1874	**11** Alex Haley born: 1921	**12** Edison invents phonograph: 1877	**13** East Germans begin building the Berlin Wall: 1961	**14** John Galsworthy born: 1867 Russell Baker born: 1925
15 Sir Walter Scott born: 1771 Panama Canal opened: 1914	**16** Transatlantic cable installed: 1858	**17** Birthday of Davy Crockett: 1786	**18** Virginia Dare born: 1587	**19** Orville Wright born: 1871 Philo T. Farnsworth born: 1906	**20** Birthday of Benjamin Harrison: 1833	**21** Hawaii enters union: 1959
22 Claude Debussy born: 1862 Ray Bradbury born: 1920	**23** Birthday of Edgar Lee Masters: 1869	**24** White House burned by British: 1814	**25** Leonard Bernstein born: 1918	**26** Amendment 19 passed: 1920	**27** Theodore Dreiser born: 1871	**28** Johann Wolfgang von Goethe born: 1749
29 Oliver Wendell Holmes born: 1809	**30** Roy Wilkins born: 1901	**31** Birthday of William Saroyan: 1908				

September

SUNDAY	MONDAY	TUESDAY	WEDNESDAY	THURSDAY	FRIDAY	SATURDAY
1 Death of Jacques Cartier: 1491-1557 World War II begins: 1939	**2** Christa McAuliff born: 1948 (d. 1986)	**3** 1st professional football game: 1895	**4** Los Angeles founded: 1781	**5** 1st Continental Congress: 1774	**6** 1st video recording on magnetic tape: 1958	**7** Grandma Moses' birthday: 1860
8 1st reading of the Pledge of Allegiance: 1892	**9** U. S. Civil Rights Act: 1957	**10** Sewing machine patented: 1846	**11** Department of War established: 1789 World Trade Center and Pentagon attaked: 2001	**12** Russians launch 1st rocket to the moon: 1959	**13** U. S. Capital established in NY: 1788	**14** Alexander von Humboldt born: 1769
15 Agatha Chrisie, James Fenimore Cooper, and William Howard Taft born	**16** Birthday of H. A. Ray, B. B. King, and John Knowles. Pilgrims sail from England: 1620	**17** U. S. Constitution signed: 1787 Work begins on Hoover Dam: 1930	**18** Birthday of Samuel Johnson: 1709 U. S. Air Force began: 1947	**19** Debut of Mickey Mouse: 1928 President Garfield died: 1881	**20** Magellan began search for passage to India: 1519	**21** Delaware becomes a state: 1776
22 Nathan Hale put to death by British: 1776	**23** Lewis & Clark comlete expedition: 1806	**24** Supreme Court founded: 1789 F. Scott Fitzgerald born: 1896 (d. 1940)	**25** Pacific Ocean discovered: 1513 William Faulkner born: 1897	**26** T. S. Eliot born: 1888 (d. 1965) George Gershwin born: 1898	**27** Thomas Nast and Samuel Adams born	**28** 1st railway locomotive runs: 1825
29 U. S. Army established: 1789	**30** 1st tooth extracted with anesthesia 1846	SEPTEMBER HAS BANNED BOOKS WEEK AND LABOR DAY.	SEPTEMBER IS LEUKEMIA AWARENESS MONTH.	SEPTEMBER IS SICKLE CELL AWARENESS MONTH.		

October

SUNDAY	MONDAY	TUESDAY	WEDNESDAY	THURSDAY	FRIDAY	SATURDAY
1 Jimmy Carter born: 1924	**2** Birthday of Ghandi: 1869 Birthday of Graham Greene: 1904	**3** Thomas Wolfe born: 1900	**4** Rutherford Hayes born: 1822	**5** Birthday of Chester A. Authur: 1830	**6** Le Corbusier born: 1887	**7** James Whitcomb Riley born: 1849 1st nuclear power plant accident: 1957
8 Don Larson pitched 1st perfect World Series game: 1956	**9** Washington Monument opened: 1888	**10** Pledge of Allegiance written: 1892	**11** Birthday of Eleanor Rooservelt: 1884	**12** Columbus lands on America: 1492	**13** White House cornerstone laid: 1792	**14** Dwight Eisenhower born: 1890 Peace Corps established: 1960 e.e. cummings born: 1894
15 Birthday of Frederick Nietzsche: 1844	**16** Noah Webster born: 1758 Oscar Wilde's birthday: 1854	**17** Birthday of Childe Hassam: 1859	**18** United States purchases Alaska: 1867	**19** Edison demonstrates electric light: 1879 Birthday of John le Carre: 1931	**20** John Dewey born: 1859 Mickey Mantle's birthday: 1931	**21** Samuel Taylor Coleridge born: 1772
22 Birthday of Michel Crichton: 1942	**23** 1st national Women's Rights Convention: 1850	**24** Anton von Leeuwenhoek born: 1632 Stock Market crash: 1929	**25** Picasso's birthday: 1881	**26** Red Cross established: 1863	**27** Dylan Thomas born: 1914 Birthday of Sylvia Plath: 1932	**28** Columbus lands on Cuba: 1492 Statue of Liberty dedicated: 1886
29 1st military peacetime draft: 1940	**30** Erza Pound born: 1885 Ballpoint pens patented: 1888	**31** Birthday of John Keats: 1795 Halloween	**OCTOBER HAS HALLOWEEN AND UNITED NATIONS DAY.**	**LIBRARY CARD SIGN UP MONTH.**	**TEEN READ WEEK IS EACH OCTOBER.**	

November

SUNDAY	MONDAY	TUESDAY	WEDNESDAY	THURSDAY	FRIDAY	SATURDAY
1 U. S. Weather Bureau established: 1870	**2** Daniel Boone born: 1734 Birthday of James Polk and Warren Harding	**3** Birthday of William Cullen Bryant: 1794	**4** King Tut's tomb discovered: 1922 Will Rogers born: 1879	**5** The Gunpowder Plot: 1605	**6** Abe Lincoln elected president: 1860 John Philip Sousa born: 1854	**7** FDR reelected for a 4th term: 1944
8 Lewis & Clark reach the Pacific: 1805 JFK elected president: 1960	**9** Berlin Wall opens: 1989	**10** Marine Corps established: 1775	**11** World War I ends: 1918 Kurt Vonnegut born: 1922	**12** First meteor shower on record: 1799	**13** Robert Louis Stevenson born: 1850	**14** Apollo 12 lifts off: 1969
15 Georgia O' Keefe born: 1887	**16** Oklahoma enters union: 1907	**17** Suez Canal opens: 1869	**18** 1st book printed in England: 1477	**19** Lincoln delivers Gettysburg Address: 1863	**20** First English child born in New England: 1620	**21** Birthday of Voltaire: 1694
22 JFK assassinated: 1963	**23** Franklin Pierce born: 1804	**24** Apollo 12 returns to earth: 1969	**25** Andrew Carnegie born: 1835	**26** FDR established modern Thanksgiving holiday: 1941	**27** America's 1st university opens: 1779	**28** Magellan reaches the Pacific Ocean: 1520
29 Louisa May Alcott born: 1832 C. S. Lewis born: 1898	**30** Mark Twain born: 1835 Brady Bill signed into law: 1993	**NOVEMBER HAS FAMILY LITERACY DAY, AMERICAN EDUCATION WEEK; AND CHILDREN'S BOOK WEEK.**	**NOVEMBER IS AMERICAN DIABETES MONTH.**			

December

SUNDAY	MONDAY	TUESDAY	WEDNESDAY	THURSDAY	FRIDAY	SATURDAY
1 English Channel finished: 1990	**2** Birthday of Seurat: 1859 Monroe Doctrine signed: 1823	**3** 1st heart transplant: 1967	**4** Phonograph invented: 1877	**5** Birthday of George Custer: 1839	**6** Microwave oven patented: 1945	**7** Japanese attacked Pearl Harbor: 1941 Willa Cather born: 1873
8 Birthday of Eli Whitney: 1765 James Thurber born: 1894	**9** Birthday of Joel Chandler Harris: 1848	**10** Birthday of Emily Dickinson and Melvil Dewey	**11** UNICEF established: 1946 Indiana admitted to union: 1816	**12** Washington, D. C. becomes capital: 1800	**13** Sir Frances Drake begins circum-navigation voyage: 1577	**14** DNA created in test tube: 1967 George Washington dies: 1799
15 Sitting Bull killed: 1890 Bill of Rights become law: 1791	**16** Birthdays of Beethoven, Jane Austen, Margret Mead, and Authur Clarke	**17** *A Christmas Carol* is published: 1843	**18** 1st performance of Tchaikovsky's Nutcracker Suite: 1892	**19** *Poor Richards's Almanack* published: 1732	**20** 1st electric incandescent light demonstrated: 1879	**21** Pilgrims land at Plymouth Rock: 1620
22 Birthday of James Olgethorpe: 1696	**23** 1st men orbit the moon: 1968	**24** Treaty of Ghent: 1814	**25** Christmas	**26** Kwanzaa	**27** Birthday of Louis Pasteur: 1822	**28** Chewing gum patented: 1869
29 Birthday of Charles Goodyear: 1800	**30** Rudyard Kipling born: 1865	**31** Birthday of Henri Matisse: 1869 1869 New Year's Eve	**THE DATE OF CHANUKAH CHANGES EACH YEAR...**	**CONSULT YOUR CALENDAR.**	**CHRISTMAS SEALS CAMPAIGN AND WORLD AIDS DAY TAKE PLACE IN DECEMBER.**	

Stencils

A a

B b

C c

Dd

Ee

Ff

Gg

Hh

Ii

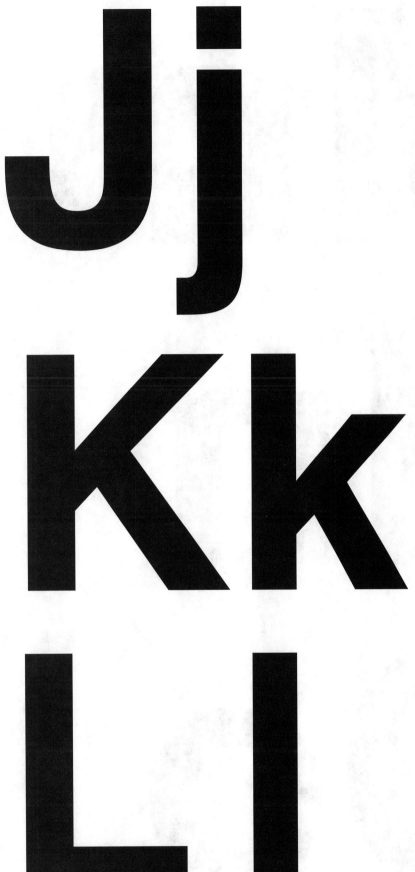

Mm

Nn

Oo

Pp

Qq

Rr

Ss

Tt

Uu

V v

W w

X x

Y y
Z z
? ! . , .

Sample Bulletin Boards

BULLETIN BOARD A

THINGS ARE LOOKING UP

AT THE LIBRARY!

BULLETIN BOARD B

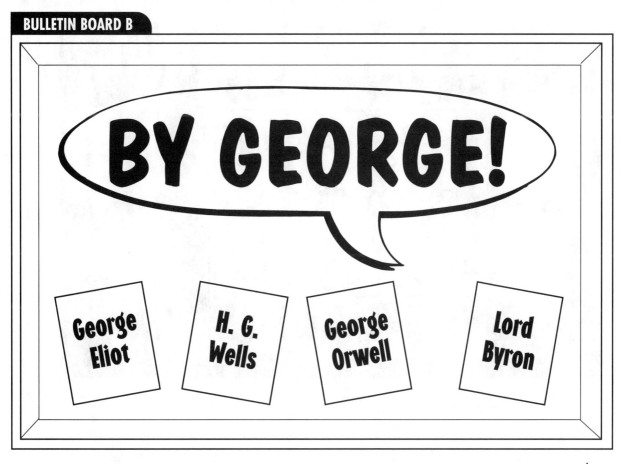

BY GEORGE!

George Eliot

H. G. Wells

George Orwell

Lord Byron

HARRY POTTER GOES TO HIGH SCHOOL

CHECK OUT THESE TITLES

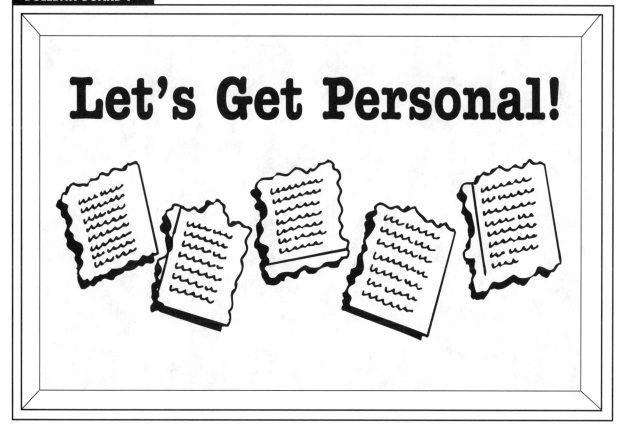

Let's Get Personal!

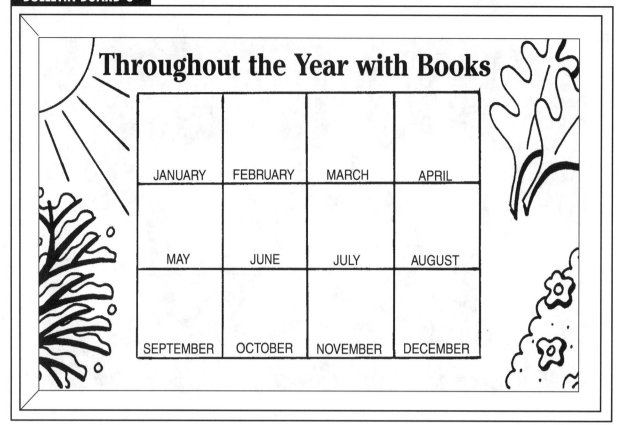

Throughout the Year with Books

JANUARY	FEBRUARY	MARCH	APRIL
MAY	JUNE	JULY	AUGUST
SEPTEMBER	OCTOBER	NOVEMBER	DECEMBER

Cameo Appearances

Who am I?   Who am I?   Who am I?   Who am I?

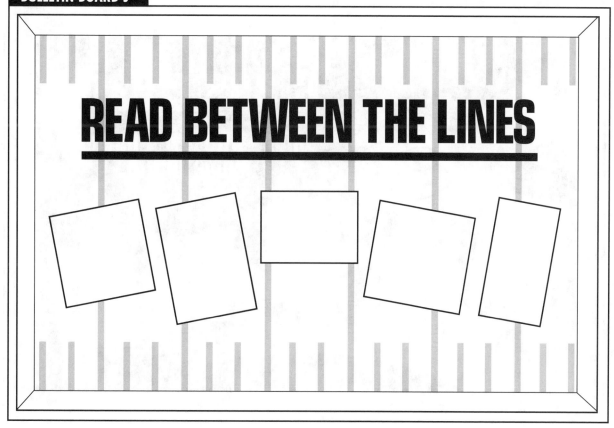

IF YOU CAN'T STAND THE

HEAT

COME INTO THE
MEDIA CENTER
AND READ A

COOL

BOOK!

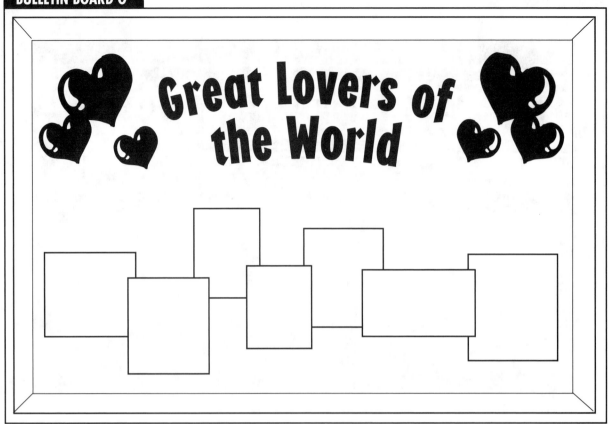

Great Lovers of the World

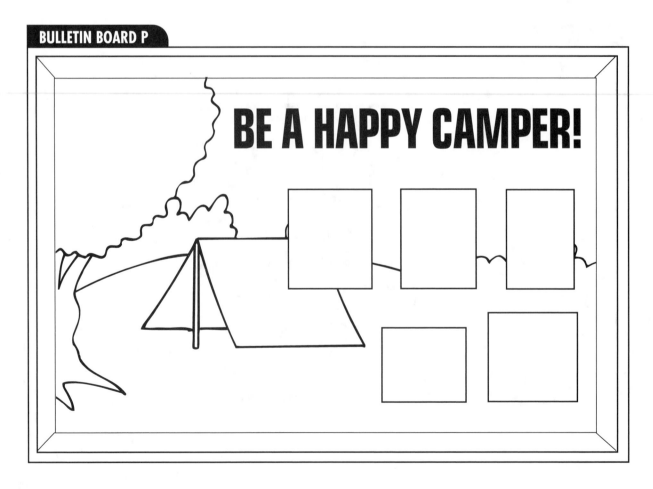

BE A HAPPY CAMPER!

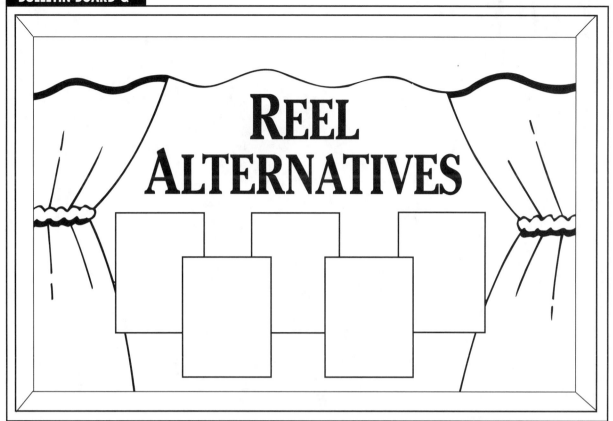

Notes

Notes